JOHN CALVIN:
HIS LIFE, HIS TEACHING, AND HIS INFLUENCE

William Wileman

GLH Publishing
Louisville, Kentucky

Originally published in 1909 by Robert Blanks and Sons.

GLH Publishing Reprint, 2019

ISBN:
  Paperback 978-1-948648-68-4
  Epub 978-1-948648-69-1

*Sign up for updates from GLH Publishing
using the link below and receive a free ebook.*
http://eepurl.com/gj9V19

CONTENTS

Preface 1
I. The Unfolding of the Purpose 2
II. Early Days of the Reformer 6
III. The Reformer's Call by Grace 11
IV. Through the Law to the Gospel 16
V. Gospel Labors in Paris 22
VI. Persecutions 25
VII. "Placards" and Martyr-Fires 31
VIII. The Institutes of the Christian Religion. ... 36
IX. A Chain of Golden Truths. 41
X. Calvin is Led to Geneva. 50
XI. Labors and Perils in Geneva. 55
XII. The Doctrines of Grace. 59
XIII. Calvin's Work at Strasburg. 64
XIV. The Reformer's Work at Geneva. 70
XV. Calvin and Servetus. 79
XVI. Influence upon England. 85
XVII. The Reformer's Last Days. 93
XVIII. Estimate of Calvin's Work. 99
XIX. Estimate of Calvin's Character. 103
XX. What the Reformation really means. 112
XXI. Our Present Position, Privilege, and Duty. 117

Preface

The following pages contain an attempt to set forth in a readable and attractive form the principal features of a great life.

While thus recording facts, the aim of the writer has been to give an honest and impartial view of those living truths of God that are commonly associated with the name of Calvin.

He has also kept in view a desire to write what should be worthy of the attention of our young people, who are warmly invited to read what God did in days of old.

I. The Unfolding of the Purpose

When God has a great work to accomplish by human instrumentality, He prepares the stage and all its surroundings, selects and equips the fittest instruments, and times their appearance. All His works praise Him; for they are founded in truth, and executed in wisdom.

Moreover, in the unfolding of His purposes, there is no evidence of hurried effort or noise. His operations are without sound of hammer. The most perfect preparation is made without halting weakness and without undue haste. The leaves of October fall from the tree not only because of their own decay, but because of the activities of the buds of the spring that is to follow. It thus occurs that the leaves and blossoms of the succeeding year are all in existence, endued with initial vigor, though as yet folded in a tiny space, some months before they fully expand to the sunlight.

Thoughts such as these crowd upon the mind in beginning to write the history of the life and times and work of John Calvin, one of the instruments selected, prepared, and used by God in effecting the Reformation.

In the fifteenth century, Rome was the metropolis of Europe. Every road on the continent led to Rome. The papacy guarded the gate of every conscience, shadowed the threshold of every home, and sat on the steps of every throne. Blind loyalty to the papal power was rewarded by a liberal supply of little bits of the "true cross," bones of saints, paper permission to commit sin, and paper pardons for sins committed.

Yet all the time the Bible was in the Vatican, hidden in Latin dust, and bound with an iron chain. The people were hungering, for the bread of life, and yearning for liberty of mind and conscience. In fact, the new buds were beginning vigorously to assert themselves, and to push away the decay and death of the centuries.

The wisdom of God is to be admired in the sequence of events which closed the fifteenth and opened the sixteenth centuries. Three important events now invite our attention. These are, first, the invention of printing; second, the birth of Luther, in 1483; third, the birth of Calvin, in 1509. It would be difficult to over-estimate the importance of these three events, or of the order in which they stand. The printing-press was necessary to any new circulation of the Bible, and thus to the spread of the gospel. It was the battering-ram to make windows in the walls of the prison, and liberate the Bible. The gospel opened the iron gates. A pathway was thus made for Luther. Sensible people shrewdly held up their parchment pardons to the light, and saw through them; yet few dared to speak their minds. It was something, however, that they had begun to think: God was even then preparing the man that would speak, and speak to purpose. The rougher work of a pioneer could not have been so well done by Calvin as by Luther; therefore God sent Luther first to clear the way.

But if Luther was a giant for valor and strength, Calvin excelled him in intellect and learning. This was necessary in the unfolding of God's plan.

In choosing the apostles, the Lord called the bold Peter before the loving John (Matthew 4:18-21); while yet designating each of the twelve to the special kind of work suited to his ability. This thought receives apt and striking confirmation from a Roman Catholic source, which may be quoted here: "It cannot be denied that Calvin was the greatest man of the Protestant rebellion. But for him Luther's movements would probably have died out with him and his associates. Calvin organized it, gave it form and consistency, and his spirit has sustained it to this day. If Luther preceded him, it is still by his name, rather than Luther's, that the rebellion should be called; and the only form of Protestantism that still shows any sign of life is unquestionably Calvinism. It is Calvinism that sustains Methodism, that gives what little it has to Lutheranism, and that prevents a very general return of Anglicans to the bosom of the church. It is hardly too much to say that no greater heresiarch than John Calvin has ever appeared, or a more daring, subtle, adroit, or successful enemy of the church of God....Considering the end of man and the purposes of civil society, murder and robbery are light crimes, and the spread of epidemic disease of no consequence, in comparison with the crime which Luther and Calvin perpetrated when they revolted from the church."[1]

After this significant testimony we may quote one stanza from the lines written by Baptist W. Noel at the time of the passing of the Maynooth Grant:

> Oh for an hour of Luther now!
> Oh for a frown from Calvin's brow!
> Once they broke the papal chain;
> Who shall break it now again?

Germany and France were foremost in the work of Reformation. While to languid Italy we owe the restoration of the arts of sculpture and of painting, and to papal Spain the discovery of a new world, we must not fail to realize that God selected Germany to produce "the smith that bloweth the coals in the fire, and that bringeth forth an instrument for his work" (Isaiah 54:16).

He entrusted to France the privilege of reviving what had been begun at an earlier date by the Albigenses and Waldenses. Switzerland was afterwards to contribute her share to the great revival; while England, who had already seen Wycliffe, the "morning-star," was to bring forth a "Noble Army" of witnesses to the living power of the grace and gospel of God.

We shall find that the unfolding of God's purpose in the Reformation was brought to pass gradually. To use the words of D'Aubigne: "The spring sun had appeared, yet winter still bound all nature in its chains; no flowers,

---

[1] These two quotations are from *The Tablet*.

no leaves, nothing that bespoke the arrival of the new season. But these appearances were deceptive; a powerful though hidden sap was already in circulation, and about to change the face of the world."

We must also remember that every reformation must first take place in the soul of the reformer before it can have any outward and manifest vitality.

If this be true as a principle of social reform, it is more nobly true of every activity in the kingdom of grace. We have before us at this period three men whom God was preparing for the great Reformation; and in each of them we trace one special and essential feature of that Reformation. Luther in great conflict of soul learned the truth that justification before God is by faith in Christ, and not, as he had been taught, by human works or merit.

Zwingli, the Reformer of Switzerland, was led, even more deeply than Luther, into the truth of the excellence and authority of Scripture. Thus we find him copying all the epistles of Paul, the manuscript of which is still preserved at Zurich. Calvin was to learn by soul-experience the doctrine of salvation by free and sovereign grace—the truth that formed the substance of his teaching through life.

These three essential principles we may call the body, soul, and spirit of the Reformation; in every point directly opposed to the teaching of the papacy. The Divine authority and pre-eminence of the Word of God; justification by faith; salvation by rich free grace. These three principles were wrought by the Holy Spirit of God in the three men entirely without any design on the part of either of them. God was the Designer; they were the instruments chosen to carry out the design. God was the Leader; it was for them to follow where He led them.

II. Early Days of the Reformer

At the threshold of the sixteenth century, a man in lowly life, by trade a *"tonnelier,"* or cooper, lived in a village named Pont l'Eveque (Bishop's Bridge in English), near Noyon, in Picardy, a province in the North of France. He had a son named Gerard Chauvin, or Cauvin, who was apostolic notary and secretary to the bishop, a position which brought no very great emolument to its holder. He lived at Noyon. Gerard Chauvin had married a young woman named Jeanne Lefranc. Their first child was a son, named Charles. The second was Jean, the subject of this history. A third son, who died in infancy, and two daughters, completed the family.

It may be convenient to state here that Jean Chauvin, in French, at a later date assumed the Latinized form "Johannes Calvinus," of which the English form is John Calvin.

John Calvin as a youth is described as of rather small stature, with keen eyes and countenance, of a studious turn, and in appearance somewhat delicate. Moreover, he seems to have inherited something of the sternness of his father; though this was modified and sweetened after his education. He himself tells us that he was "of a disposition somewhat unpolished and bashful, which led me always to love the shade and retirement." He adds to this: "I began to seek some secluded corner where I might be withdrawn from the public view; but so far from being able to accomplish the object of my desire, *all my retreats were like public schools.* In short, whilst my one great object was to live in seclusion without being known, God so led me about through different turn-

II. Early Days of the Reformer

ings and changes, that He never permitted me to rest in any place until, in spite of my natural disposition, He brought me forth to public notice."

He was thus born with a love of retirement, study, and the pursuit of learning; and, it need scarcely be added, most devotedly attached to the superstitions of the Church of Rome.

Gerard Chauvin was desirous that his children should receive the best possible education. In his position as bishop's secretary he became familiar with the noble family of De Mommor, and the young Jean was brought up with Claude Mommor, receiving the same education. By this early training he not only acquired a good foundation of learning, but also received a higher degree of cultivation than was possible for him at home.

It is impossible here not to be reminded of the similar preparation for his lifework of Saul of Tarsus, afterwards the apostle Paul, of whose learning God had designed to make use, as well as of his capacity to labor and to suffer for the gospel. The hand of God is in all biography as well as in all history.

It is evident that from a very early age Calvin was filled with reverence for God, and worshipped Him, though yet in much darkness, yet with a devoutness almost beyond his years. One author, though not naming his authority, records that it was Jean's custom, while very young, to worship God in the open air. But perhaps this was merely his interpretation of Calvin's statement, just quoted, that he loved the shade and retirement. Yet it is quite likely; for God was about to grant to him larger mews than those of the Roman Church, and to lead him into the liberty of the gospel.

His education being somewhat beyond his father's means, Gerard wished to have his son attached to the church, with the view of his advancement in its service. When Jean was twelve years of age, the chaplaincy of a small church, named La Gesine, became vacant; and the father sought from the bishop the benefit of his patronage and help on behalf of his son. It should be said in explanation that in those times it was quite a common practice to bestow ecclesiastical titles and offices upon mere children.

Thus we read of one who was made a cardinal at eight years of age, and of another at eleven, by Clement VII. This fact must account for the otherwise so remarkable an occurrence at so early a date in Jean's life.

The bishop conferred the desired appointment on May 21, 1521; and Jean Chauvin was made the Chaplain of Gesine. We are bound to trace in this event certain links in the chain of God's providence. His father was in favor with the bishop of Noyon, and with his vicar-general, and could thus present and press his petition; and God, having a favor to the lad, was leading him by a way that he knew not to a position far higher than his father could have pictured or would have desired.

For two years did the youthful chaplain live at Noyon, holding his benefice at La Gesine, but without fulfilling any of its duties, of which in the nature of things he was not capable. In that little town was born a man in whose heart bubbled up "rivers of living water," (John 7:38) which in due time flowed forth to fertilize many a barren place, and to gladden many a thirsty soul. "In the last day" of the Feast of Tabernacles, when the boughs were withered, "that great day of the feast, Jesus stood and cried, saying, If any man thirst, let him come unto Me, and drink. He that believeth on Me, as the Scripture hath said, out of his belly shall flow rivers of living water." (John 7:37-38) The youth had been for about two years in possession of his title when a terrible plague—in those days not uncommon—visited that part of France.

The "black pestilence" broke forth, and caused great alarm to the inhabitants of the towns and villages. The priests in terror fled from their duties; and Gerard Chauvin, feeling afraid for his son, sought and obtained permission for Jean to leave the district. He asked for "leave to go whither his mind should lead, without loss of his emoluments." This permission was given in August, 1523, when the youth was fourteen years of age.

At this juncture the De Mommors were proceeding to Paris to continue their studies; and it was arranged

II. Early Days of the Reformer

that Jean Chauvin should go with them; thus securing his safety, and at the same time filling the heart of his father with pleasant visions of his advancement in learning and in the church. The canon of Noyon, in recording this event, says: "In flying from the pestilence here, he went to catch another infection elsewhere."

The young students entered the college of La Marche, which at that time, as Beza tells us, had a very remarkable teacher named Mathurin Cordier, a man of refined taste and of considerable acquirements. In all this we still trace the unfolding of the Divine purpose towards Calvin.

A new world was thus opened to the young student. He saw spread before him the rich stores of Latin literature, which he made his own by diligent study with apparent ease. A mutual trust and regard grew between the great teacher and the greater scholar; and the scholar drank deeply from the streams which so refreshed his ardent mind. Cordier could not teach Calvin the truth of God, for himself, alas! was a stranger to its power; but God was watching over the working out of His own design, even in these preparatory exercises of learning the classics and of acquiring facility of speech and of argument. And thus what Gamaliel was to Saul of Tarsus at Jerusalem, Cordier was to Calvin of Noyon at Paris. Nor should we omit here to record that what Luther did for the German language, and what our own Reformers did for the English, that Calvin did for the French. The gospel ennobles everything it touches, exalts every nation that shelters it, and enriches every language that speaks and spreads it. The three languages, German, French and English, are richer today for the influences brought to bear upon them by Luther, Calvin, and the Reformers.

The young student fulfilled his term of study at La Marche, and entered college in 1526, at the age of seventeen. The college chosen was that of Montaigu, then high in reputation for the training of students intended for the "priesthood." How the new student progressed at his new school may be expressed in the testimonies of more than one historian; Protestants and Romanists agreeing in the verdict.

Bossuet says: "Luther triumphed orally, but the pen of Calvin was more correct. Both excelled in speaking the language of their country."

Etienne Pasquier testifies: "Calvin was a man who wrote well...to whom our tongue is greatly indebted." "No one of those who preceded him," says Florimond de Raemond, "excelled him in writing well; and few since have approached him in beauty and felicity of language."

It was thus that Moses was "learned in all the wisdom of the Egyptians" (Acts 7:22) before he chose "rather to suffer affliction with the people of God" (Hebrews 11:25).

It was thus that Paul learned earthly wisdom in the school of Gamaliel, which, when sanctified and ennobled by grace, was to be of so great use to him, before he was taught the knowledge of salvation in the school of Christ. The man, in fact, was being fitted for the work to be given him to do, as will be seen in due course.

III. THE REFORMER'S CALL BY GRACE

The time was now approaching for a thirst for a higher wisdom to be implanted in the soul of young Calvin. Tenderly, reverently, and not without feeling, have the words "call by grace" been placed at the head of this chapter. Who that has passed through this vital crisis, variously described though the somewhat differing terms in essence mean the same—as regeneration, conversion, the new birth, and effectual calling, can record it, of himself or of another, without emotion, without devout and holy gratitude? Who can even look back to the dawning of eternal life in his own soul without humbled admiration and chastened joy? There was a time, even now not remote, when it was common to use the expression "effectual calling" to describe the fact of "passing out of death into life" (John 5:24; 1 John 3:14); the fact ascribed by Paul to the sovereign grace of God: "And you hath He quickened, who were dead in trespasses and sins" (Ephesians 2:1).

The time, the appointed time, for producing this change in the soul of Calvin was drawing near, all unknown to himself. There is a singular beauty; as well as a singular force, in that word "yet" in Acts 9:1: "And Saul, *yet* breathing out threatenings and slaughter against the disciples of the Lord."

As much as to imply: the hour is coming, and is very near, though he knows it not, when Saul shall breathe prayers instead of threatenings. This is the hour indicated by Jesus in John 5:25: "The hour is coming, and now is, when the dead shall hear the voice of the Son of God; and they that hear shall live."

We should like to know much more than we do of the secret working of the Spirit of God in the conversion of Calvin. I have perused the principal of the many biographies of the Reformer; but all of them are deficient on this point. Here and there, in his Prefaces to his Commentaries, and more fully in his Letters, we find just such scattered details as make us long for more. But, weighing all these accounts, there are, as I judge, three chief facts that stand out most prominently above all others, and in which we must now proceed to trace the co-working of God's providence and grace.

There is, first of all, *what is always first,* and always at the beginning least perceived by its subject, the secret drawing of the Holy Spirit of God.

Whatever open facts in one's outward life, whatever special occurrences of providential leading, this is assuredly the central mainspring, the efficient motive-power, that governs and guides all of them. And as one principal object of these pages is to magnify the free grace of the great Author of life, it is fitting that this object be plainly avowed on this early page, though it will be expanded in a later chapter.

Then, second, descending from the fountain to the stream, from the secret purpose to the open operations, there would be the effect produced by the martyrdoms which at that time were causing many minds in Paris to ponder. We do not certainly know that Calvin saw the burning of James Pavanne or of the hermit of Livry; but whether so or not, he must have been conversant with the feeling of the people with regard to these and other martyrdoms, and must have formed an opinion as to the meaning of them.

But, third, and this can be more clearly traced, there was the intimacy of Calvin with his countryman and cousin, Robert Olivetan, who was afterwards to have the honor of being one of the first to preach the "new doctrine" at Geneva, and who was one of the first by whom Calvin heard it preached. It is very evident that the conversations between the two relatives were used by the Spirit of God to lead Calvin into the light of day and into

III. THE REFORMER'S CALL BY GRACE

the liberty of the gospel.

The fires which burned the martyrs led the cousins to discuss the two religions. Robert took the side of God and truth; John defended the "church" and himself. The battle proceeds from day to day. There is no sign of victory for either side at first. The arguments used by Olivetan are drawn from the Word, and must prevail at length; but the logical mind of John Calvin was not one that would readily yield to argument. Any new thought must be slowly assimilated, and weighed in all its aspects. It could accept nothing as proved until the proof was clear and absolute. But one advantage of this careful analysis and severe testing would be that whatever was once accepted would remain unmovable. *"There are only two religions in the world."* This appears to have been the sword-thrust from the lips of Olivetan which silenced his cousin. He persisted in showing that one religion was invented by man, and consisted in the supposed merit of good works; and that the religion that came from God was wrought in the heart by God Himself as its Author and Finisher.

In plain terms, he pleaded that salvation is entirely of grace, through faith, not of works, but the gift of God. *"There are only two religions in the world."* What was true four hundred years ago is true today. In the seventh of Matthew are *seven* solemn contrasts. Two gates—strait and wide; two ways—narrow and broad; two trees—good and corrupt; two kinds of fruit—good and evil; two builders—wise and foolish; two foundations—rock and sand; two houses—the one that stood and the one that fell. Happy the man who by divine grace has the first of these two religions. Reader, *have you?*

The arrow of conviction having thus by the hand of the Holy Spirit been fixed in the heart and conscience of the young student, *none but the same hand could draw it out.* Calvin could not comfort himself, nor would he accept comfort from his cousin. But Olivetan did all he could to persuade Calvin to study the Scriptures. While this to us at this day seems trite advice, we must remember that at that date it was not so easy to follow it, besides the danger incurred in doing so. But God continued to show him more clearly every day that there was no salvation by the works of the law or by human merit; that the law could only curse him, and that his own works were defiled and dead. *Herein was the whole of the Reformation being enacted first in the soul of the Reformer.* It is ever so.

None but a saved sinner can preach salvation by grace; none but a crucified man can preach a crucified Christ. "Every time I went down into myself," he tells us of this conflict, "or raised my heart to God, so extreme a horror fell upon me that no purifications, no satisfactions, could cure me of it. And the more closely I considered myself, the sharper were the goads that pressed my conscience, so that there remained no other comfort than to forget myself."

True indeed for John Calvin and for every burdened and oppressed sinner, struggling under the pain and pressure of conviction of sin. It is only in looking away from self, and looking to Jesus, that the burden rolls from the heart.

In this trouble of soul, Calvin went to the Bible. He opened, he read, he discovered. As he continued to open the Word, it was opened to his renewed understanding. As he read, it was read to him by its Author. As he discovered its holy doctrines, they were applied to him by the hand that wrote them. In them he learned this essential truth: "Neither is there salvation in any other; for there is none other name under heaven given among men, whereby we must be saved" (Acts 4:12).

At length the day dawned, and the darkness fled away. As he read and looked away from self, he came to this: "But He was wounded for our transgressions; He was bruised for our iniquities; the chastisement of our peace was upon Him; and with His stripes we are healed" (Isaiah 53:5).

By the application of this word he "received the atonement," joyfully believing in Jesus. "O Father," he responded, "His sacrifice has appeased Thy wrath; His blood has washed away my impurities; His cross has borne my curse; His death hath atoned for me!"

On *that* day salvation came to *that* heart (Luke 19:9), and the Reformation in France was begun. The entrance of God's words gave light to Calvin, and lighted a candle that is burning to this day.

IV. THROUGH THE LAW TO THE GOSPEL

We make a brief pause in our narrative in beginning this chapter to glance at what was then taking place in Paris. The sun of the gospel had indeed risen in France, and devouted men were preaching with much success; but France had not given the same heartiness of welcome to the truth that had been accorded by Germany. God deals with nations as with individuals: any measure of rejection of light is followed by a judicial withdrawal of the measure of light given. While Luther was saying "No" to the pope and the papacy in Germany, France was preparing to say "No" to the gospel; and she has never ceased to reap the fruit of that denial.

Among the diligent teachers of the truth in Paris at this time were Lefevre and Farel. Their great desire and hope were that Francis I, the French king, should place his influence on the side of the Reformation. A good desire, in itself; but God had higher thoughts than theirs. While they were praying for the conversion of Francis, God was bringing to pass the conversion of a young student of whose existence they were ignorant. This student was to wield a mightier influence than could have been exercised even by the throne of France. The Bible, the gospel, the truth, the prison, the martyr-fire; these were what God was about to use in preference to the power of a throne, the smiles of a court, the sunlight of royal protection.

Two very important facts now present themselves to our attention, intended by God to exert an influence over the whole future of the Reformer's life. These are, first, a storm of doubts in his mind as to the "church";

IV. Through the Law to the Gospel

and, second, his father's desire that his studies should henceforth be with a view to follow the law and forsake the priesthood. It is not a little remarkable that Luther's father also intended his son for the law. God's purpose in the case of Luther and in the case of Calvin, and in the cases of many obscurer servants of His since their day, was infinitely higher and better than theirs.

With regard to the first of these facts, we must remember that every exercise of Calvin's mind must be subjected to the most rigorous examination of his subtle intellect. He could accept nothing without being convinced of its logical consistency with truth. He therefore could not renounce his faith in the Romish church without first finding a better faith and a better church. Not rashly, therefore, for his mental disposition was timid and retiring, did he cast himself into a path of conflict with his native opinions. His predilections were all on the side of quiet study and repose.

But he had begun to inquire and to seek for truth, and could not rest short of finding it. The one thing he wanted was to know what was *truth*. Could he find that, he would be content to follow wherever it might lead him. He cared little for man's judgment.

Two powers now strove for victory. On the one hand, he began to give hesitating heed to the suggestion: "Would it not be better to renounce these enquiries, and remain in the old stream of thought, believing as others do? Wherefore cast myself into this agony, at the risk of gaining nought but persecution?" On the other hand, he was impelled by the motive implanted in him when he passed out of death into life. This power, this motive, this voice, in the end gained the victory, because eternal life was at its root: He continued to study the Bible, possibly the translation into French which Olivetan was then making.

The second fact was his father's desire for Calvin to study law. His own account of this is so beautiful as a piece of autobiography, and so characteristic of the writer, that I quote it in full. It occurs in his Preface to the Commentary on the Psalms.

> But as he [David] was taken from the sheepfold, and elevated to the rank of supreme authority; so God having taken me from my originally obscure and humble condition, has reckoned me worthy of being invested with the honorable office of a preacher and minister of the Gospel. When I was as yet a very little boy, my father had destined me for the study of theology. But afterwards, when he considered that the legal profession commonly raised those who followed it to wealth, this prospect induced him suddenly to change his purpose. Thus it came to pass, that I was withdrawn from the study of philosophy, and put to the study of law. To this pursuit I endeavored faithfully to apply myself, in obedience to the will of my father; but God, by the secret guidance of His providence, at length gave a different direction to my course.
>
> And first, since I was too obstinately devoted to the superstitions of popery to be easily extricated from so profound a depth of mire, God by a sudden conversion subdued and brought my mind to a teachable frame, which was more hardened in such matters than might have been expected from me at my early period of life.
>
> Having thus received some taste and knowledge of true godliness, I was immediately inflamed with so intense a desire to make progress therein, that although I did not altogether leave off other studies, I yet pursued them with less ardor. I was quite surprised to find that before a year had elapsed, all who had any desire after purer doctrine were continually coming to me to learn, although I myself was as yet but a mere novice and tyro.

We therefore now view the Reformer as for a time drawn aside from the pursuit of truth through the study of the Word to the pursuit of worldly advancement by the study of the law. "The design of making him a priest," says Beza, "was interrupted by a change in the views of both father and son. In the former, because he saw that the law was a surer road to wealth and honor; in the latter, because having become acquainted with the reformed faith, he had begun to devote himself to the

IV. Through the Law to the Gospel

study of Holy Scripture; and from an abhorrence of all kinds of superstition to discontinue his attendances on the public services of the church."

He therefore proceeded to Orleans, to study law under Pierre de l'Etoile, one of the first French lawyers of that period. Here he made rapid progress. The historian Raemond tells us that he distinguished himself by "an active mind and a strong memory, with great dexterity and promptness in gathering up the lessons and sayings which fell from his master's lips, noting them down afterwards with marvelous facility and beauty of language." To this Beza adds: "At the end of a year, he was no longer considered as a scholar, but as a teacher." In fact, he was more than once asked to supply his master's place.

But the digression was not yet at an end. A jurist of repute at Milan, Andrew Alciati, had been summoned by Francis I to the academy at Bourges, and had received much honor. Attracted by his reputation, Calvin went to Bourges, to sit at the feet of Alciati. Here he studied as few had done before him, giving the closest application to his master's lectures each evening, and committing them to memory and to writing on the following mornings.

While thus laboriously learning law at Bourges, the Reformer met another teacher, Melchior Wolmar, who was to lead him back into the path he had left.

Wolmar was a professor of Greek; and while openly teaching Homer, he did not hesitate to teach the Greek of another Book, which he had brought from Germany. "In this book," he would say, "is the answer to every problem, the remedy for every abuse, the rest of every heavy-laden soul."

It was under this influence while at Bourges that Calvin began to preach the gospel of Christ. Those who heard the young man expound the Scriptures "heard him gladly," and entreated him to become their minister.

He replied, "I have hardly learned the gospel myself, and lo! I am called to teach it to others."

His first attempts were made in the town of Bourges,

and thence carried to the surrounding villages, especially one named Lignieres, where he was much encouraged by a wealthy man and his lady. His method was to go from house to house, and, opening the Bible, to explain its messages in the simplest manner to his hearers. His teaching thus dropped like rain and distilled as the dew. His pure doctrine, thus issuing fresh from the very fountain of life, was most refreshing to his thirsty hearers. His manner was gentle and sweet, so that all were attracted by this youthful preacher of the "new doctrine."

While thus pursuing his gospel labors, a message from Noyon, informing him of the death of his father, called him from them. But having planted, another was raised up to water, named Michel Simon.

In his journey to Noyon, the Reformer "must needs go through" Paris.

God had there something for him to see and to ponder. One of the noblest sons of France was about to lay down his life for the testimony of Jesus Christ; and it was necessary for Calvin to be a witness to his death. It was a further lesson in the school of truth.

Louis de Berquin belonged to a noble family of Artois. He was devoted to study, beloved by all, and a favorite at court. But, having a dispute with one of the Sorbonne doctors on a point of theology, he went to the Bible, and found what he had not expected. He found that the "new" doctrine was the true doctrine. His conversion was marked; and from that hour his eloquence and zeal were devoted to the gospel. This drew upon him the malice of his associates. As they could not silence him by argument, they tried to silence him in another way. Three times was he apprehended; and on each occasion liberated by order of Francis.

At length an incident occurred that brought him within their power. An image of the Virgin at a street-corner was so helpless to defend itself as to be mutilated; and this was charged upon Berquin's teaching. He was arrested, imprisoned, tried, and sentenced to death; and in the absence of the king, to whom he had appealed, the doctors hurried the execution of their sentence. At noon on April 22nd, 1529, Berquin was led forth to die.

Arrived at the Place de Greve, he stood beside the stake, and asked permission to speak to the people. But the monks denied his request, and at a signal given by them the martyr's voice was drowned by clash of arms. "Thus," says Felice, "the Sorbonne of 1529 set the populace of 1793 the base example of stifling on the scaffold the sacred words of the dying." *God never forgets.*

The little heap of the ashes of Berquin appeared, to the eyes of foes and friends, the grave-mound of the Reformation in France. But the purposes of God survive many deaths; and are never buried except to rise again.

V. Gospel Labors in Paris

We may well believe that the death of Berquin filled the heart of the young evangelist on his way to Noyon with thoughts of sorrow. He had been absent from his native place for six years; he returns a young man of twenty, the same pale-faced student, yet vitally changed. He is received by the townsmen with differing feelings.

The church at Pont l'Eveque was readily opened to him; and there, in the hearing of those who had known him as a boy, he expounded the Scriptures. The results were exactly as recorded in those living pages, true in all times and places: "And some believed the things which were spoken, and some believed not" (Acts 28:24).

He himself relates of this period that God "led him and whirled him about," so as to leave him no repose in any place whatever, till "He had brought me into the light and into action." This will doubtless explain to us why Calvin stayed only about two months in his native town. God had a larger sphere for him to fill; and when this is the case, God leads His servants by a way that they knew not. Even opposing circumstances concur with those that seem favorable to bring to pass what He ordains.

We therefore follow the Reformer back to Paris, which was at this time the seat of the government of France, the center of learning, and the theater of much disputation and strife about truth. The "old" and the "new" doctrines met in daily conflict, and were eagerly discussed by men in all ranks of society. Calvin knew *both* systems; and was therefore capable of entering into the arguments on both sides with the advantage always thus attaching to experience. Besides, his naturally astute and logical mind had been disciplined by his legal studies; while at the same time, it had been sanctified and sweetened by the entrance of the gospel. It is most evident that, in choosing Paris for his abode, the Reformer was led by God into the sphere most fitted for him and for the work he was to accomplish.

He took up his abode in the house of a merchant, Etienne [Stephen] de la Forge, who was an ardent lover of the truth, and who was afterwards burned for his attachment to it. Calvin speaks of this good man as one "whose memory ought to be blessed among believers as a holy martyr for Christ." It was in this house that Calvin began to hold assemblies for preaching, at first privately, afterwards more openly. It is to be remarked that at this early period the Reformer concluded all his discourses with the words: "If God be for us, who can be against us?" This reveals to us that he had counted the cost, and that he was determined in the strength of God to go forward in the path he had chosen. Of this fact a French writer of the period gives the following striking testimony, the more remarkable because a Roman Catholic: "Devoted otherwise to his books and his study, he was unweariedly active in everything which concerned the advancement of his sect. We have seen our prisons gorged with poor, mistaken wretches, whom he has exhorted without ceasing, consoled or confirmed by letters; nor were messengers wanting, to whom the doors were open, notwithstanding all the diligence exercised by the jailers. Such were the proceedings by which he commenced, and by which he gained, step by step, a part of our France. Thus it went on till, after a considerable length of time, seeing men's minds disposed to his cause, he wished to proceed more rapidly, and to send us ministers, called 'preachers,' to promulgate his religion in holes and corners, and even in Paris itself, where the fires were lit to consume them."[2]

Our heartiest thanks to this historian for his noble tribute to the already ardent, yet unobtrusive labors

---

[2] The latter is from the issue of January 27th, 1877. Pasquier, Recherches de la France, page 769.

of our Reformer. Quiet, untiring, laborious zeal in the cause of the gospel marked the preacher's movements in these early days.

In 1532, Calvin issued his first publication from the press, a Commentary, in Latin, on the "De Clementia of Seneca." I have referred to a copy of this book, and find it signed on the title-page: *"Lucius Calvinus civis Romanus."* From this time he laid aside his French name, Chauvin, and became known as Johannes Calvinus. The majority of Calvin's biographers have somewhat stumbled at this publication, no doubt feeling that it was a departure from his gospel work. Many of them, therefore, seek to excuse it on the ground that he wished to induce the king to manifest less severity against the Protestants, and more "clemency" towards the gospel. After carefully weighing the arguments for and against this view, I may venture to express an opinion. The author himself says nothing of the kind, either at the time or later, in his Letters or his Prefaces. I rather judge that we have in this book one of those noted instances wherein God was at work unseen, bringing to pass "His bright designs" out of darkness. The work was a masterpiece of writing, in the most elegant Latin, and at once procured much fame for its author.

Attention was drawn to the man as well as to the book; and *the reputation of the man of letters was to prepare the way for the Reformer.* Paul's early education often in later days secured him an audience as a preacher; and thus it was to be with Calvin. His "Commentary" on Seneca would make men read his "Commentaries" on Scripture when they should see the light in days to come.

These days of Gospel seed-sowing were perhaps the quietest of Calvin's life. Avoiding disputations with the Sorbonne doctors, and quietly going with "the Book" from door to door, he won many a soul from the kingdom of darkness to the realm of light and truth. Dark clouds, however, were gathering on the horizon; and thunders were muttering in the distance, the signs of an approaching storm.

VI. Persecutions

It will be convenient at this stage to give an outline of the condition of France at this period.

Francis, the king, was no real friend to Protestantism. He had not the love of the truth in his heart. We therefore find him at one time persecuting the Protestants, and at another favoring them. But in either case his motive would be one of state policy. He was anxious to check any designs of the papacy that would thwart his designs or cripple his power. This made him hold out one hand to the Reformers of Germany, and the other to Henry VIII of England.

Margaret de Valois, queen of Navarre; was his sister, and had known and favored Calvin at Bourges. She had read the Bible, and its truths had been explained to her by the aged Le Fevre.

She was occupying the palace and court during the absence of Francis in Picardy after the festivities of Lent; and resolved to have the "new" doctrine preached in the churches of Paris. A movement in favor of the gospel was thus begun in the highest quarter; while Calvin was quietly working among the people. Margaret summoned Gerard Roussel to her presence, and commanded him to preach the glad tidings of salvation from the pulpits of the city. Roussel hesitated; and the Sorbonne doctors raged and opposed. But Margaret persisted in her design. She had a chapel prepared in the Louvre, and had it publicly announced that the gospel would be preached daily therein.

Thus sheltered by the protection of the king and queen of Navarre, and by the royal roof, Roussel preached daily; and thousands listened to the tidings of salvation by grace. It looked as if the gospel had achieved a mighty triumph.

Margaret, encouraged by the success of her plan, wrote to ask the consent of Francis to the opening of the churches in the city. He named two of them in his reply. These churches were filled with hearers, and numbers received the gospel with great joy.

As might have been foreseen, all this called for intense and bitter opposition. Priests and monks and doctors united to inflame the people against the queen and her preachers. For a time, this opposition only fanned the gospel flame, and spread its conquests. But only for a time, as we shall presently see; for other flames were already being kindled.

As Roussel enjoyed the protection of the court, another victim must be found by the doctors. A Dominican friar, Laurent de la Croix, had been wrought upon by the gospel in Paris. He proceeded to Geneva, to be there instructed in the truth by Farel. But, yearning for the salvation of his countrymen, he crossed the frontier, taking the name of Alexander, and went to Lyons. Here he preached with such manifest power that many were called by grace out of darkness into marvelous light. At length he was arrested, and sent to Paris. After enduring much cruel torture, he was sentenced to be burned alive. Though unable to walk to the place of execution, as one leg was crushed, he preached Christ to the people as he was conveyed to his death. The onlookers said, "He is going to be burned; yet no one is so happy as he. Surely there is nothing worthy of death in this man. If he is not saved, who then can be?"

This was the day of France's visitation. The Gospel came to France, and asked for admission. France said *No*. The result was its withdrawal. The Divine law is that a willful rejection of the Gospel, with light and privilege, shall be followed by judicial blindness. France has from that day to this reaped the sad harvest according to her own refusal. As with individuals, whatsoever nations sow, so they also must reap.

Calvin was an interested, but a silent, spectator of these stirring events.

VI. Persecutions

Four years of reading, study, prayer, retirement, were needful for the coming conflicts. Invited to meet Margaret at the Louvre, he might have obtained preferment at her hands, when a storm broke suddenly upon Paris and upon Calvin.

The rector or head of the College of the Sorbonne, Nicholas Cop, had come under the influence of the truth; and although yet in much twilight, was advancing to the day. On the "octave of Martinmas," November 1st, 1533, Cop, as the rector, according to custom, was to give the annual oration.

Calvin perceived herein a favorable opportunity of bringing the truth before the doctors and students of the college. He waited on Cop, and laid this before him; but the doctor felt unequal to the occasion, or was afraid to venture. It was agreed that Calvin should write, and that Cop should read, such an address as should answer the intention. Calvin "framed for him," says Beza, "an oration very different from what was customary."

Yes, very different, indeed. A brilliant assembly of students, doctors, and citizens met on the day. Cop rose, and delivered an oration which exalted the grace of God. The merit of human works was roughly handled, and justification by faith prominently taught. The grace of God, in short, was preached as the one fountain of life, pardon, and salvation.

The effect was unmistakable. Many a countenance beamed with delight.

Astonishment, joy, wrath, might be plainly read on the faces of the listeners. Nothing like it had ever before been heard on the festival of La Toussaint.

Suspicion as to the authorship of the oration fell on Calvin. Neither the Parliament nor the Sorbonne could allow it to pass uncensured. Cop was summoned to appear, and was arrested; but, managing to escape, he fled to Basle. Officers were then sent to the College of Fortret, where Calvin was sitting quietly, to arrest him. Warned of their approach, and urged to fly, he escaped, according to some accounts, by being let down, like Paul, from a window. In any case, he escaped; and, as Desmay narrates, he ran to St. Victor, and exchanged clothes with a vine-dresser. His papers were seized and searched, and several of his friends named therein had also to flee.

Turning southward, the Reformer went towards Orleans, thence to Tours; and proceeding further, after wandering for some weeks, reached Angouleme, the birthplace of Margaret of Navarre. Here he bent his steps to the mansion of Louis Du Tillet, a canon of the town, of a noble and wealthy family. This canon had traveled much, and the mansion possessed a library of nearly four thousand volumes, for that day an immensely rich collection.

No one was better fitted or inclined than our fugitive for the repose of this hospitable mansion, or for the enjoyment of this library. He did not fail to drink deeply from its streams. He repaid Du Tillet for his kind reception by teaching him Greek, which certainly meant teaching him the gospel.

According to the Roman Catholic historian, Raemond, it was in this library that Calvin, "in order to entrap Christendom, first wove the web of his *Christian Institutes,* which we may call the Koran, or rather the Talmud, of heresy." It is very true, Raemond; and we heartily thank you for this and other honest confessions of yours.

The beloved apostle was banished by the heathen emperor to the Isle of Patmos for his testimony to the truth; and there received from his Lord the letters to the seven churches and the Revelation of God's purposes to the end of time. Luther, during his detention in the Wartburg, translated the New Testament into German. Rutherford wrote his heavenly letters from Aberdeen. Bunyan wrote his "immortal" works in Bedford jail. And there can be no question that John Calvin spent six months to good purpose among the four thousand volumes in the library of his friend and protector.

The historian Henry says, "it must have been now that he prepared the first sketch of the *Institutions."* To which Bayle adds: "Some say that he composed the greater part of his *Institutions* at Claix, in the house of

VI. Persecutions

Louis Du Tillet." Claix is a village near Angouleme, of which Du Tillet was curate.

Traces of the Reformer's stay here long existed. A vineyard known as "Calvin's Vineyard" was so named as late as 1714.

The *Institutes* will require our attention in a separate chapter.

While at Angouleme, Calvin visited Le Fevre, the veteran preacher, at Nerac. It was Le Fevre who had said to Farel, "My dear Guillaume, God will renew the face of the world, and *you* will see it." The meeting of the aged and the young reformers was most touching. Calvin admired the ripeness of the aged saint: Le Fevre was charmed by the promise of the young man. Beza tells us that the veteran took his young brother by the hand, and said "Young man, you will one day be a powerful instrument in the Lord's hand. God will make use of you to restore the kingdom of heaven in France."

After this much needed and much enjoyed rest of six months at Angouleme, the Reformer retraced his steps northward, and went to Poictiers. Here he gathered round him a congregation of willing and thirsty hearers, including the chief magistrate. At first they met for worship in a garden; but afterwards, for greater secrecy and safety, in a cave in the rocks near the river, then known as the "Cave of Benedict," but from that day to this as "Calvin's Grotto." Here he preached, and here the company worshipped. Here also he administered the Lord's Supper, as is believed for the first time in France, in its Scriptural order, *in two kinds,* that is, both bread and wine. This requires the explanation that at the Council of Constance, in 1414, it was decreed that no priest, under pain of excommunication, should communicate to the people under both kinds.

The priests were to drink the wine; and the people might partake of the bread.

After a sojourn of two months at Poictiers, Calvin went boldly to Paris by way of Orleans. It was his plan, his intention, his desire, that Paris should be the scene and center of his labors; God's plan and intention was leading him in another direction. Calvin did not then perceive that Paris had invited and incurred judicial darkness by rejecting the light. It is no cause for wonder to us now that he so desired Paris. Some of us have survived our dearest hopes and sweetest anticipations; and have lived to pluck the fairest flowers from the graves of our stricken joys. The hand that thrice led Calvin out of Paris was guiding him surely to his life-work.

VII. "Placards" and Martyr-Fires.

Persecution was not dead in Paris, though somewhat held in check by the influence of Margaret. She had obtained from Francis the concession that the lovers of truth should be "left more tranquil"; but Jean Morin had not forgotten John Calvin, and was burning for revenge.

Calvin left Poictiers at the end of April, 1534. He was therefore approaching the age of twenty-five, when, according to the canons, he must enter the priesthood. He was still nominally in the church of Rome, though his heart was freed from her servitude. The time approached for his decision. On the left hand was the path of expediency; on the right hand the path to wealth and position. Straight before him was the path of loyalty to Christ. He chose this.

In pursuance of his choice, he went at once to Noyon, where, on May 4th, 1534, he resigned his chaplaincy of La Gesine, and his curacy of Pont l'Eveque. In addition to this public act, he sold his paternal inheritance, and thus severed on the same day his connection with his native town and his native church. We need not stay here to remark how completely these free acts furnish a reply to those historians who impute shameful motives to his first departure.

Having thus severed the last link that bound him to Rome, he returned to Paris, where he made a brief stay, to leave it for the last time.

It was on his return to Paris that Calvin first met a man whom he was to meet on a later day at Geneva,—Michael Servetus. As a few pages will be specially required later for a review of this man's case, so far as it relates to Calvin, I need only say here in passing that Servetus was a Spaniard, born in the same year as our Reformer. He had just issued a book on the Trinity, and challenged Calvin to a discussion of its teaching. This challenge was accepted. The day, the time, the place for the discussion were agreed upon; but, for some reason that has never seen the light, Servetus failed to appear.

Calvin now returned to his former lodging in the house of Antoine de la Forge, in the Rue St. Denis. Here he resumed his quiet labor by going from house to house, and preached in the home of his worthy host. A few of his friends must be introduced here, as we shall find them shortly led forth to suffer at the stake.

Near La Forge's dwelling was a shoemaker's shop, where a poor deformed dwarf sat day by day, named Bartholomew Millon. As the result of a fall, this poor creature became bent and paralyzed, while his mental powers retained their former rigor. It was his delight to ridicule and insult the Protestants who passed his shop. One of these, touched with pity, stopped and said, "Poor man, do you not see that God has bent your body in order to straighten your soul?" With this kind word, he handed the cripple a New Testament, asking him to read it. The result was his conversion. His humble shop from that time became a center from which went forth the truth of God. He taught young people to read, and charmed many by singing Marot's Psalms.

Another friend of truth was John du Bourg, a draper, a man of some position. He was visited by Peter Valeton, who thus came under gospel influence. Other members of this Protestant band were Le Compte and a bricklayer named Henry Poille.

Yet Calvin found no opening, as he had hoped, for continuous gospel labor; and it is likely that he felt the approach of the tempest that was so soon to burst. He therefore resolved to go to Germany; and, probably in July, 1534, accompanied by Du Tillet, he left Paris. The two travelers reached Strasburg in safety.

They had not been long out of Paris when the threatened storm broke. His departure was timely; for had he

VII. "Placards" and Martyr-Fires.

remained in Paris for a few weeks longer, he would have been numbered among the victims of the storm.

It was in October that an outbreak of indiscreet zeal on the part of some friends of the Reformation inflicted a severe blow upon the cause of truth, and called forth severe repressive measures.

A servant of the king's apothecary, Peter Feret, was sent to Neufchatel, in Switzerland, to confer with the Swiss Reformed pastors. They were asked whether it was not time for them to arise and make some bold open stand for God and truth.

The result of this conference was a decision to prepare a placard, to be brought into France and posted in the most public places. This placard was most intemperately worded. The authorship has been ascribed to Farel; but Bungener says that "the author has never been known." I have referred to the original, as given by Gerdesius and Paul Henry; and none of us would approve the use of such terms as "apostates, false pastors, wolves, blasphemers, execrables," etc. The wrath of man is misguided in such a channel as this. An army of men posted copies of this fiery document in the most public places of Paris during the night of October 18th. It should be said that the authors of this placard, however just and true its contents, wrote only what the Swiss believed; but they forgot that the scathing words of the manifesto would be more calculated to inflame the papists of France than to convince them of their errors. One of the papers was posted at the Louvre; another on the door of the king's chamber.

As might have been foreseen, Francis was highly incensed at this audacity.

Two things now became urgent: to punish those who had been guilty of the outrage; and to purge the city of the pestilence. We must very briefly narrate how these were effected.

The king gave orders for the arrest of the prominent Protestants; and Jean Morin was glad to obey. Du Bourg, the merchant, Bartholomew Millon, the cripple, Valeton, Poille, and some others were arrested; and after a hasty trial were on the 10th November sentenced to death, the sentence to be carried into effect within three days. The circumstances of the burning of these faithful witnesses, their speeches at the stake, their triumphant joy in the flames, and the effect produced on the populace, would make an interesting chapter; but it would occupy too much of our space.

Roussel and the other preachers employed by Margaret were apprehended and imprisoned, but their lives were spared at her request, and they escaped from the city.

Having thus punished the more prominent of those who were supposed to have favored the "placards," it was resolved to offer some public reparation for the insult to the church. On January 21st, 1535, an imposing procession was formed, in which every available priest was included; and the "host," with much splendor and ceremony, followed by the king, was carried to Notre Dame in the presence of thousands of spectators. After "mass" had been performed, the king made an oration, in which he pledged himself to root out the Protestant heresy to the utmost of his power. Immediately the fires began again to blaze in the public places of Paris; and numbers of witnesses of the truth were first brutally tortured and then burned.

France little thought, on that fatal January 21st, 1535, that another and yet another 21st of January would witness scenes yet more dreadful. On January 21st, 1793, another king—Louis XVI—formed part of a procession to the block and to death. And, within the memory of some of us, on January 21st, 1871, Paris, after a siege of four months, capitulated to the victorious German army.

As we have seen, Calvin escaped this fiery tempest. He set out with Du Tillet on the road to Germany, hoping to find there a place of rest. The travelers halted at Strasburg, but could not there discover either an opening for the gospel or any friendly welcome. After a sojourn there of a few months, they passed on to Basle, the gateway into Switzerland.

It was at this juncture, early during his stay at Basle,

that Calvin had an interview with the great scholar Erasmus. He had rendered a great service to the cause of the Reformation by the publication of the New Testament.

But he was less a Reformer than a scholar. His idea was more that of a reformation *in* the church than *of* the church. He was more fitted for the flower-border than for plowing and spade-work. To use a modern expression, he was a "trimmer," trying to find a middle course and thus escape the cross. He was not the man to do and dare for Christ, to suffer and die for the truth. Calvin therefore found in Erasmus little that was after his own heart, and no union was formed between them.

Halfway men are hinderers rather than helpers. Whole-hearted service is what the Lord looks for and rewards with His approving smile. The Lord's message to Polycarp in Revelation 2:10: "Be thou faithful unto death, and I will give thee a crown of life," does not mean faithful *until* death, but, as it really was in his case, *unto* death.

In Basle Calvin hoped to find the seclusion he so longed for. He took up his abode in the house of Catherine Klein, a good woman who harbored many a servant of Christ in exile, and who perceived and valued the nobility of the exile she now had the honor to shelter. In this quiet retreat Calvin pursued his studies; and here he produced the first edition of his great and undying work, *The Institutes of the Christian Religion,* which next invites our attention.

VIII. The Institutes of the Christian Religion.

We have seen on a previous page that the inception of the *Institutes* took place in the Angouleme library. Some biographers think that the first draft was written there; others take the contrary view. But we are upon safe ground in tracing the birth of this great work. In his retirement in Basle, Calvin heard of the fierce persecutions of the Reformed in Paris, of the "placards," and of the burnings. He would remember the martyrs as his brethren. And now also he would hear the bitter and cruel charges that were made against them falsely by their enemies; and his whole great soul went forth to vindicate them and the gospel they loved. Many a noble and beautiful tree has grown from the ashes of the martyrs. One of the most entrancing beauties of nature I have ever gazed upon, and I have seen it more than once, is the sheets of cherry-blossom just outside Coventry, covering some acres of the ground on which God's witnesses left their ashes and their blood. So the *Institutes* grew out of the fire.

We have his own testimony to this. I quote from his Preface to the Psalms:—

> Whilst I lay hidden at Basle, and known only to a few people, many faithful and holy persons were burned alive in France; and the report of these burnings having reached foreign nations, they excited the strongest disapprobation among a great part of the Germans, whose indignation was kindled against the authors of such tyranny. In order to allay this indignation, certain wicked and lying pamphlets were circulated, stating that none were treated with

such cruelty but erroneous and seditious persons, who, by their perverse ravings and false opinions, were overthrowing not only religion but also all civil order. Observing that the object which these instruments of the court aimed at by their disguises, was not only that the disgrace of shedding so much innocent blood might remain buried under the false charges and calumnies which they brought against the holy martyrs after their death, but also that afterwards they might be able to proceed to the utmost extremity in murdering the poor saints without exciting compassion towards them in the breasts of any, it appeared to me that, unless I opposed them to the utmost of my ability, my silence could not be vindicated from the charge of cowardice and treachery. *This was the consideration which induced me to publish my Institute of the Christian Religion.* My objects were, first, to prove that these reports were false and calumnious, and thus to vindicate my brethren, whose death was precious in the sight of the Lord.

And next, that as the same cruelties might very soon after be exercised against many unhappy persons, foreign nations might be touched with at least some compassion towards them and solicitude about them. When it was then published, it was not that copious and labored work which it now is, but only a small treatise containing a summary of the principal truths of the Christian Religion; and it was published with no other design than that men might know what was the faith held by those whom I saw basely and wickedly defamed by those flagitious and perfidious flatterers. That my object was not to acquire fame appears from this, that immediately after I left Basle; and particularly from the fact that nobody there knew that I was the author. Wherever else I have gone, I have taken care to conceal that I was the author of that performance.

Two things are apparent from this noble extract, which I could not curtail: that God had a higher design than Calvin; and that what he so tried to conceal was destined to come to the light. I have counted no fewer than thirty-seven editions of the *Institutes* in the British

Museum catalogue.

The first edition was written in Latin, and was published at Basle, in 1536.

It contained six chapters. The second edition, 1539, comprised seventeen chapters. The edition of 1543 consisted of twenty-one chapters; and the completed edition of 1559, eighty-four.

Speaking of the growth of the book, the author says:—"Though I had no cause to be displeased with my labor in the matter, nevertheless I do confess that I had no satisfaction in it till I had digested it into its present order, which I hope you will approve...I spared myself all the less till I had completed the book, which, surviving after my death, might show how desirous I was to satisfy those who had already found profit in it...I had wished to do it sooner; but it will be soon enough if well enough; and for myself it will suffice that it has borne fruit to the church of God."

How much fruit, and how rich, only the great day will reveal.

The style is simple, correct, clear, elegant, animated, and varied in form and tone. His pen is ready, flexible, and skillful in expressing all the shades of thought and feeling.

During the remainder of his life, the author devoted himself to the expansion of his work; which thus grew, not like a building, but like a tree.

Twenty-seven years of his life formed the preparation to write it; twenty-seven years were employed by him in enlarging and completing it. The first translation was into French; and it was afterwards translated into most of the languages of Europe.

We should expect that the orderly mind of Calvin would produce a book modeled in perfect method. This is so; and, like all sound method, it is simple.

The author divides his work into four parts. The knowledge of God the Father; faith in God the Son as Redeemer; the Person and work of God the Holy Spirit; and the church of God.

The preface is addressed to Francis I, King of France,

VIII. THE INSTITUTES OF THE CHRISTIAN RELIGION. 39

and is dated "Basle, 1st August, 1536." A quotation from this preface will be interesting to the reader. "My intention was to furnish a kind of rudiments, by which those who feel some interest in religion might be trained to true godliness. And I toiled at the task chiefly for the sake of my countrymen the French, multitudes of whom I perceived to be hungering and thirsting after Christ, while very few seemed to have been duly imbued with even a slender knowledge of him. But when I perceived that the fury of certain bad men had risen to such a height in your realm that there was no place in it for sound doctrine, I thought it might be of service if I were in the same work both to give instruction to my countrymen, and also lay before your majesty a Confession, from which you may learn what the doctrine is that so inflames the rage of those madmen who are this day, with fire and sword, troubling your kingdom."

From the "Epistle to the Reader," prefixed to the second edition, published at Strasburg in 1539: "When I perceived that almost all the godly had received it with a favor which I had never dared to wish, far less to hope for, being sincerely conscious that I had received much more than I deserved, I thought I should be very ungrateful if I did not endeavor, at least according to my humble ability, to respond to the great kindness which had been expressed towards me, and which urged me to diligence."

From the preface to the French edition, published at Geneva, 1545: "And since we are bound to acknowledge that all truth and sound doctrine proceed from God, I will venture boldly to declare what I think of this work; acknowledging it to be God's work rather than mine. I exhort all who reverence the word of the Lord to read it, and diligently imprint it on their memory. When they shall have done so, they will know by experience that I have not wished to impose upon them with words."

A brief extract from the "Epistle to the Reader," prefixed to the last edition that was revised by the author: "Though I do not regret the labor previously expended, I never felt satisfied until the work was arranged in the order in which it now appears. Now I trust it will approve itself to the judgment of all my readers. As a clear proof of the diligence with which I have labored to perform this service to the church of God, I may be permitted to mention that, last winter, when I thought I was dying of quartan ague, the more the disorder increased, the less I spared myself, in order that I might leave this book behind me, and thus make some return to the godly for their kind urgency....Farewell, kind reader; if you derive any benefit from my labors, aid me with your prayers to our heavenly Father.—*Geneva,* 1st *August, 1559."*

The teaching of John Calvin has been so misrepresented by the opponents of the great doctrines of grace, as well as by the papists, and also so misunderstood even by some who profess to embrace them, that in my judgment it will serve a useful purpose to give a careful selection of Calvin's own thoughts in his own words. This will answer many questions and instruct the questioners. It sometimes occurs that opposers know very little of what they oppose; and we have very good authority and example for "in meekness instructing those who oppose themselves."

To prevent the growth of this chapter unduly, I will devote a separate chapter to a concise view of the *Institutes.*

IX. A Chain of Golden Truths.

Extracts from the *Institutes*.

In laying before the reader an outline of the *Institutes*, the course I have decided to follow is both methodical and simple. I shall give extracts from Calvin's great work, arranged in a manner that is likely to be very helpful to every reader; hoping also that it will be useful for reference. The advantage of this is obvious. It is allowing the author to speak for himself.

The selection of these extracts has been the most laborious contribution to this book; but in all such labor there is profit.

Instead of availing myself of the labors of others, I have carefully read the *Institutes* for the purpose of making the following selections:—

1. THE HOLY SCRIPTURES. "Let it therefore be held as fixed, that those who are inwardly taught by the Holy Spirit acquiesce implicitly in Scripture; that Scripture, carrying its own evidence along with it, deigns not to submit to proofs and arguments, but owes the full conviction with which we ought to receive it to the testimony of the Spirit. Enlightened by Him, we no longer believe, either on our own judgment or that of others, that the Scriptures are from God; but, in a way superior to human judgment, feel perfectly assured as much so as if we beheld the divine image visibly impressed on it— that it came to us, by the instrumentality of men, from the very mouth of God. We ask not for proofs or probabilities on which to rest our judgment, but we submit our intellect and judgment to it as too transcendent for

us to estimate."

2. THE FALL OF MAN. "It cannot be doubted that when Adam lost his first estate he became alienated from God. Wherefore, although we grant that the image of God was not utterly effaced and destroyed in him, it was, however, so corrupted, that anything which remains is fearful deformity; and, therefore, our deliverance begins with that renovation which we obtain from Christ, who is, therefore, called the second Adam, because He restores us to true and substantial integrity."

3. CORRUPTION OF HUMAN NATURE. "It is necessary only to remember, that man at his first creation, was very different from all his posterity; who, deriving their origin from him after he was corrupted, received a hereditary taint. At first every part of the soul was formed to rectitude. There was soundness of mind and freedom of will to choose the good. If anyone objects that it was placed, as it were, in a slippery position, because its power was weak, I answer, that the degree conferred was sufficient to take away every excuse. For surely the Deity could not be tied down to this condition—to make man such, that he either could not or would not sin. Such a nature might have been more excellent; but to expostulate with God as if He had been bound to confer this nature on man, is more than unjust, seeing He had full right to determine how much or how little He would give. Why He did not sustain him by the virtue of perseverance is hidden in His counsel; it is ours to keep within the bounds of soberness. Man had received the power, if he had the will, but he had not the will which would have given the power; for this will would have been followed by perseverance. Still, after he had received so much, there is no excuse for his having spontaneously brought death upon himself. No necessity was laid upon God to give him more than that intermediate and even transient will, that out of man's fall He might extract materials for His own glory."

4. THE PROVIDENCE OF GOD. "Hence, our Savior, after declaring that even a sparrow falls not to the ground without the will of His Father, immediately makes the

IX. A Chain of Golden Truths.

application, that being more valuable than many sparrows, we ought to consider that God provides more carefully for us. He even extends this so far, as to assure us that the hairs of our head are all numbered. What more can we wish, if not even a hair of our head can fall, save in accordance with His will? I speak not merely of the human race in general. God having chosen the Church for His abode, there cannot be a doubt, that in governing it, He gives singular manifestations of His paternal care. But when once the light of Divine Providence has illumined the believer's soul, he is relieved and set free, not only from the extreme fear and anxiety which formerly oppressed him, but from all care. For as he justly shudders at the idea of chance, so he can confidently commit himself to God. This, I say, is his comfort, that his heavenly Father so embraces all things under His power—so governs them at will by His nod—so regulates them by His wisdom, that nothing takes place save according to His appointment; that received into His favor, and entrusted to the care of His angels, neither fire, nor water, nor sword can do him harm, except in so far as God their Master is pleased to permit."

5. THE SOVEREIGN WILL OF GOD. "Their first objection—that if nothing happens without the will of God, He must have two contrary wills, decreeing by a secret counsel what He has openly forbidden in His law—is easily disposed of. But before I reply to it, I would again remind my readers that this cavil is directed not against me, but against the Holy Spirit, who certainly dictated this confession to that holy man Job, 'The Lord gave, and the Lord hath taken away,' when, after being plundered by robbers, he acknowledges that their injustice and mischief was a just chastisement from God. And what says the Scripture elsewhere?"

6. GOD NOT THE AUTHOR OF SIN. "In the same way is solved, or rather spontaneously vanishes, another objection viz., If God not only uses the agency of the wicked, but also governs their counsels and affections, He is the Author of all their sins; and therefore men, in executing what God has decreed, are unjustly condemned, be-

cause they are obeying His will. Here *will* is improperly confounded with *precept,* though it is obvious, from innumerable examples, that there is the greatest difference between them."

7. ORIGINAL SIN. "How far sin has seized both on the mind and heart, we shall shortly see. Here I only wish briefly to observe, that the whole man, from the crown of the head to the sole of the foot, is so deluged, as it were, that no part remains exempt from sin, and, therefore, everything which proceeds from him is imputed as sin. Thus Paul says, that all carnal thoughts and affections are enmity against God, and consequently death (Romans 8:7). Let us have done, then, with those who dare to inscribe the name of God on their vices, because we say that men are born vicious. The divine workmanship, which they ought to look for in the nature of Adam, when still entire and uncorrupted, they absurdly expect to find in their depravity. The blame of our ruin rests with our own carnality, not with God, its only cause being our degeneracy from our original condition. And let no one here clamor that God might have provided better for our safety by preventing Adam's fall. This objection, which, from the daring presumption implied in it, is odious to every pious mind, relates to the mystery of predestination, which will afterwards be considered in its own place (*Tertull. de Praescript. Calvin, Lib. de Predest.*). Meanwhile, let us remember that our ruin is attributable to our own depravity, that we may not insinuate a charge against God Himself, the Author of nature."

8. PREDESTINATION. "When we attribute foreknowledge to God, our meaning is, that all things have always been under His eyes, and His sight, as present. And we call predestination the eternal decree of God, whereby He determined with Himself what He would have to become of every man. For men are not created to like estate; but for some eternal life, and for some eternal death, is appointed. Whereby His free election is made manifest, seeing it lieth in His will, what shall be the estate of every nation. Whereof God showed a token in the whole issue of Abraham. There is also a certain special election,

IX. A Chain of Golden Truths.

wherein appeareth more plainly the grace of God, seeing that of the same stock of Abraham God rejected some, as Ishmael, Esau, and at length almost all the Ten Tribes of Israel."

9. FREE WILL. "In this way, then, man is said to have free will, not because he has a free choice of good and evil, but because he acts voluntarily, and not by compulsion. This is perfectly true: but why should so small a matter have been dignified with so proud a title? An admirable freedom! that man is not forced to be the servant of sin, while he is, however, ἐθελοδουλος (a voluntary slave); his will being bound by the fetters of sin. I abominate mere verbal disputes, by which the Church is harassed to no purpose; but I think we ought religiously to eschew terms which imply some absurdity, especially in subjects where error is of pernicious consequence. How few are there who, when they hear free will attributed to man, do not immediately imagine that he is the master of his mind and will in such a sense, that he can of himself incline himself either to good or evil? It may be said that such dangers are removed by carefully expounding the meaning to the people. But such is the proneness of the human mind to go astray, that it will more quickly draw error from one little word, than truth from a lengthened discourse. Of this, the very term in question furnishes too strong a proof."

10. USE OF EXHORTATIONS. "Still it is insisted, that exhortations are vain, warnings superfluous, and rebukes absurd, if the sinner possesses not the power to obey. When similar suggestions were urged against Augustine, he was obliged to write his book, 'De Correptione et Gratia,' where he has fully disposed of them. The substance of his answer to his opponents is this: 'O, man! learn from the precept what you ought to do; learn from correction, that it is your own fault you have not the power; and learn in prayer, whence it is that you may receive the power.'...But it will be asked, why are they now admonished of their duty, and not rather left to the guidance of the Spirit? Why are they urged with exhortations when they cannot hasten any faster than

the Spirit impels them? and why are they chastised, if at any time they go astray, seeing that this is caused by the necessary infirmity of the flesh? 'O, man! who art thou that repliest against God?' If, in order to prepare us for the grace which enables us to obey exhortation, God sees meet to employ exhortation, what is there in such an arrangement for you to carp and scoff at? Had exhortations and reprimands no other profit with the godly than to convince them of sin, they could not be deemed altogether useless. Now, when, by the Spirit of God acting within, they have the effect of inflaming their desire of good, of arousing them from lethargy, of destroying the pleasure and honeyed sweetness of sin, making it hateful and loathsome, who will presume to cavil at them as superfluous?"

11. UNIVERSAL AND SPECIAL CALLING. "There is a double kind of calling, universal, whereby God, through the outward preaching of the Word, biddeth all men come to Him, as well good as evil. And there is also another special calling, whereof, for the most part He vouchsafeth the faithful only, which He bringeth to pass by the inward illumination of the Spirit, so that the Word preached doth take root, and settle in their hearts; and yet He doth sometimes make those also partakers thereof, whom He doth illuminate only for a season; then afterwards He forsaketh them for their unthankfulness, and striketh them with greater blindness."

12. THE SUFFERINGS OF CHRIST. "To such a degree was Christ dejected, that in the depth of His agony He was forced to exclaim, 'My God, My God, why hast Thou forsaken Me?' The view taken by some, that He here expressed the opinion of others rather than His own conviction, is most improbable; for it is evident that the expression was wrung from the anguish of His inmost soul. We do not, however, insinuate that God was ever hostile to Him or angry with Him. How could He be angry with the beloved Son, with whom His soul was well pleased? or how could He have appeased the Father by His intercession for others if He was hostile to Himself? But this we say, that He bore the weight of the divine

IX. A Chain of Golden Truths.

anger; that, smitten and afflicted, He experienced all the signs of an angry and avenging God."

13. RESURRECTION OF CHRIST. "Our salvation may be thus divided between the death and the resurrection of Christ: by the former, sin was abolished and death annihilated; by the latter, righteousness was restored and life revived, the power and efficacy of the former being still bestowed upon us by means of the latter. Paul accordingly affirms, that He was declared to be the Son of God by His resurrection (Romans 1:4), because He then fully displayed that heavenly power which is both a bright mirror, of His divinity, and a sure support of our faith; as he also elsewhere teaches, that 'though He was crucified through weakness, yet He liveth by the power of God' (2 Corinthians 13:4). In the same sense, in another passage, treating of perfection, he says, 'That I may know Him and the power of His resurrection' (Philippians 3:10). Immediately after he adds, 'being made conformable unto His death.' In perfect accordance with this is the passage in Peter, that God raised Him up from the dead, and gave Him glory, that your faith and hope might be in God' (1 Peter 1:21)."

14. CHRIST THE JUDGE. "It is most consolatory to think, that judgment is vested in Him who has already destined us to share with Him in the honor of judgment (Matthew 19:28); so far is it from being true, that He will ascend the judgment-seat for our condemnation. How could a most merciful prince destroy his own people? How could the head disperse its own members? How could the advocate condemn his clients? For if the Apostle, when contemplating the interposition of Christ, is bold to exclaim, 'Who is he that condemneth?' (Romans 8:33), much more certain is it that Christ, the Intercessor, will not condemn those whom He has admitted to His protection. It certainly gives no small security, that we shall be sisted at no other tribunal than that of our Redeemer, from whom salvation is to be expected; and that He who in the Gospel now promises eternal blessedness, will then as Judge ratify His promise. The end for which the Father has honored the Son by committing all judg-

ment to Him (John 5:22), was to pacify the consciences of His people when alarmed at the thought of judgment."

15. THE HOLY SPIRIT'S WORK. "We must now see in what way we become possessed of the blessings which God has bestowed on His only begotten Son, not for private use, but to enrich the poor and needy. And the first thing to be attended to is that so long as we are without Christ and separated from Him nothing which He suffered and did for the salvation of the human race is of the least benefit to us. To communicate to us the blessings which He received from the Father He must become ours and dwell in us. Accordingly He is called our Head, and the first-born among many brethren, while, on the other hand, we are said to be ingrafted into Him and clothed with Him, all which He possesses being, as I have said, nothing to us until we become one with Him. And although it is true that we obtain this by faith, yet since we see that all do not indiscriminately embrace the report of Christ which is made by the Gospel, the very nature of the case teaches us to ascend higher, and inquire into the secret efficacy of the Spirit, to which it is owing that we enjoy Christ and all His blessings."

16. REPENTANCE. "God, indeed, declares that He would have all men to repent, and addresses exhortations in common to all. Their efficacy, however, depends on the spirit of regeneration. It were easier to create us at first than for us by our own strength to acquire a more excellent nature. Wherefore, in regard to the whole process of regeneration, it is not without cause we are called God's 'workmanship, created in Christ Jesus unto good works, which God hath before ordained that we should walk in them' (Ephesians 2:10). Those whom God is pleased to rescue from death He quickens by the spirit of regeneration; not that repentance is properly the cause of salvation, but because, as already seen, it is inseparable from the faith and mercy of God, for, as Isaiah declares, 'The Redeemer shall come to Zion, and unto them that turn from transgression in Jacob.' This, indeed, is a standing truth, that wherever the fear of God is in vigor the Spirit has been carrying on His saving work."

IX. A Chain of Golden Truths.

We may fitly close this selection of holy truths by simply adding the *"golden* chain" of Romans 8:—"And we know that all things work together for good to them that love God, to them who are the called according to His purpose. For whom He did foreknow, He also did predestinate to be conformed to the image of His Son, that He might be the first-born among many brethren. Moreover, whom He did predestinate, them He also called; and whom He called, them He also justified; and whom He justified, them He also glorified." (Romans 8:28-30)

X. Calvin is Led to Geneva.

In February, 1536, Calvin went to Italy, with the purpose of visiting the court of Ferrara. Here the duchess Renee gave encouragement and protection to persecuted Protestant exiles. We have few details of this visit. Calvin afterwards said that he entered Italy only to leave it again. In spite of an assumed name (Charles d'Espeville) the officers of the Inquisition appear to have recognized him, and he fled from their tender mercies. Beza, however, seems to imply that he left Ferrara of his own will, being required at Noyon on the death of his brother Charles. In any case, he went to Noyon and settled the family affairs, leaving it this time forever. Where shall he now go?

No doubt remembering Basle, with his brother Antoine and his sister Maria, he left his native place to go to Basle. The way through Lorraine was closed by the war. The travelers arrived at Geneva in July, 1536.

Calvin took his lodging in the house of Peter Viret, one of the ministers of that city, intending to stay there only a single night.

But his Master had designed that Geneva should be the scene of his future work.

It is necessary here to make a brief digression in our narrative, in order to take a survey of the events immediately preceding Calvin's arrival there.

William Farel had for some years been preaching the gospel there. Many had been his conflicts, labors, and persecutions.

Geneva had been the scene of many contests. Situated as it was, it formed a convenient center for the refugees who were driven chiefly from France for the gospel's sake. In 1524 the Genevese threw off the authority of the duke of Savoy; and many were impatient to rid

X. Calvin is Led to Geneva.

themselves of the yoke which bound them to Rome.

In 1532 Farel and Saunier entered Geneva, and worked with Robert Olivetan, the cousin of John Calvin. A council was called, and Farel was condemned to be banished. A tumultuous mob basely ill-treated him, threatening him with death. One man attempted to shoot him, and pulled the trigger, but it missed fire. Farel turned to him, and said, "I am not to be shaken by a popgun; your toy does not alarm me."

Farel and his companions were ordered to leave the town within six hours, or be burned. But he was not the man to be easily turned aside. He was soon back in Geneva, and with Froment preaching and teaching.

Many disturbances occurred when it was found that Farel and Froment, like Peter and John, had returned; the relation of which would swell our narrative unduly. In 1535 an attempt was made to poison the three preachers, Farel, Viret and Froment; but although the poison was in the soup, Farel changed his dish, Froment was called away, and Viret alone took some, the effects of which remained with him through life.

The Reformers next entered the churches and broke down the images.

These gods of wood and stone were unable to help themselves. On this, the Council took the matter in hand, and decreed that the "mass" should be abolished. The priests then sent to inform the duke of Savoy of the state of matters; and the result was a holy war.

Deliverance came to Geneva on February 2nd, 1536. The gospel was victorious, and the city was free.

On May 21st, the Council called together the citizens, and put it to them whether they would decide for popery or for the gospel. After a deep silence, in a loud and solemn voice came the answer: "We all, with one accord, desire, by God's help, to live in the faith of the holy gospel, and according to God's Word, as it is preached to us." Then the people, with uplifted hands, responded: "We swear to do so. We will do so, by God's help."

The Council then ordered an inscription to be placed over one of the city gates, and afterwards over the entrance to the town hall, that all might see how God had delivered them. The following is a translation: —

> The tyranny of the Roman Antichrist
> Having been overthrown,
> And its superstitions abolished in the year 1535,
> The most holy religion of Christ
> Having been restored,
> In its truth and purity,
> And the church set in good order,
> By a signal favor of God;
> The enemy having been repelled
> And put to flight,
> And the city by a striking miracle
> Restored to liberty;
> The senate and the people of Geneva have erected
> And set up this monument,
> In this place,
> As a perpetual memorial,
> To attest to future ages
> Their gratitude to God.

By this the Reformation of Geneva was established; but the victory was not yet complete. These worthy laborers needed a helper; one, moreover, who would seek to advance the cause by his voice and pen without clamor. *This helper was even now on his way to them.*

One evening in July, 1536, Calvin arrived, as we have seen, at Geneva. He thought of reposing there for a night, and departing on the morrow. His presence was discovered by either Caroli or Du Tillet, and at once made known to Farel.

Farel was thankfully surprised at the good news. He had read the *Institutes,* and now the author was within reach. In establishing the Reformation in Geneva, Farel had been unable to hold in check the fiery zeal of some, the lawlessness of others, the errors of yet others. He therefore perceived at once what an acquisition to himself and to the cause of truth would this young man be.

The story of their meeting has been variously narrated. I will write it from not fewer than six sources.

Farel waited upon the traveler, and pointed out to

him what had been taking place in Geneva. He then showed him what a field was here opened before him for Gospel labor; and invited the student and author to join him.

Calvin shrank from the prominence and the responsibility, and frankly said so. He loved retirement, and wished rather to write than to preach. He was merely passing through the city; he needed rest; and other arguments. "But why seek elsewhere for what is now offered you here? Why refuse to edify the church of God by your faith, knowledge, and zeal?" "I cannot teach; I have need to learn. There are special labors for which I wish to reserve myself. This city cannot afford me the leisure I require." "Study, leisure, knowledge!" replied Farel, "Must we never practice?"

Calvin further objected the fiery zeal of some in Geneva, and his own timidity and need of rest. "Rest! death alone releases the servants of Christ from their labors. Ought they to be so delicate as to be afraid of warfare? Jonah wanted to flee from the presence of the Lord, but the Lord cast him into the sea!"

Then Farel could restrain himself no longer. Rising from his seat, and placing his hand on Calvin's head, and fixing his eyes on him, he said, "Then God will curse your repose, and your studies, if in so dire a necessity as ours, you withdraw, and refuse to give your help and support." "Then I will remain at Geneva. I will give myself up to the Lord's good pleasure."

From that precious mine of autobiography, the Preface to the Psalms, I extract a sentence in Calvin's own words confirming this narration: "I had resolved to continue in the same privacy and obscurity, until at length William Farel detained me at Geneva, not so much by counsel and exhortation, as by a dreadful imprecation, which I felt to be as if God had from heaven laid His mighty hand upon me to arrest me. As the most direct road to Strasburg, to which I then intended to retire, was shut up by the wars, I had resolved to pass quickly by Geneva, without staying longer than a single night in that city. Then an individual who now basely apostatized and returned to the papists [Caroli is meant] discovered me and made me known to others. Upon this Farel, who burned with an extraordinary zeal to advance the gospel, immediately strained every nerve to detain me. And after having learned that my heart was set upon devoting myself to private studies, for which I wished to keep myself free from other pursuits, and finding that he gained nothing by entreaties, he proceeded to utter an imprecation that God would curse my retirement and the tranquility of the studies which I sought, if I should withdraw and refuse to give assistance, when the necessity was so urgent."

From that time he cast himself heart and soul into the work of the gospel.

He had already by his pen done the work of a lifetime; he was now to enter upon a second lifetime of labor, a brief outline of which now awaits our attention.

XI. Labors and Perils in Geneva.

Thus brought by the providence of God into his new sphere, Calvin at once associated himself with Farel and the other pastors.

Soon after his arrival, he was chosen teacher of theology, at first declining the office of preacher, which he undertook in the following year. As he had often preached at Bourges and elsewhere, this singular backwardness at his age (twenty-seven) can only be understood by supposing that he trembled at the solemnity and burden of the work. "Who is sufficient for these things?"

His earliest labors seem to have been moderately paid. In February, 1537, we find a proposal to pay him "six gold crowns, seeing that he has hitherto received scarcely anything." After a time, he preached in the Cathedral, and his eloquence attracted many hearers.

In October, we find Calvin, Farel, Viret, Fabri, Caroli, and others, attending a disputation which the Council of Berne had appointed to be held at Lausanne. Vigorous attempts were made to prevent this conference; but they were discovered and frustrated.

On the fourth and fifth days Calvin addressed the gathering on transubstantiation. A friar, named Tandi, confessed himself at once a convert to the reformed doctrine, and threw off his monk's frock, never to be worn again. Farel rose, and said, "Let us thank our Lord together. Let us receive our new brother, for whom Christ has died, as Christ has received us."

This conference proved of great service in advancing the Reformation cause.

Farel and Calvin drew up a Confession of Faith,

containing twenty-one articles; the nineteenth of which claimed the power to excommunicate unholy and vicious persons until repentant. On November 10th, 1536 this Confession was laid before the Council of Two hundred, who ordered it to be printed, publicly read, and circulated.

At this point a trouble arose, caused by Caroli, This man had been a doctor of the Sorbonne, and had professed conversion to the "new" doctrines. He was vain, weak, fickle, changing his opinions with every wind for the sake of advantage. By these unworthy means rising step by step, he made an attempt to obtain the office of inspector over the churches. But the Council perceived his pride, and suitably rebuked him.

This so mortified him that he meditated vengeance on the pastors, and he selected the more prominent to accuse them of Arianism. The defense of Calvin is so noble that I quote part of it: "It is but a few days ago that I dined with Caroli. I was then his very dear brother, and he told me to make his compliments to Farel. He then treated as brethren those whom he now charges as heretics, and protested that he wished always to live in brotherly love with us. But not a word did he say about Arianism. Where was then the glory of God? Where the purity of the faith, and the unity of the church? If you had a single spark of true zeal or piety, would you have silently suffered your brethren and colleagues to reject the Son of God? Would you soil yourself with the infection of such an impiety by communicating with them? But, supposing all this of no consequence, I demand how you know that I am infected with the Arian heresy. I believe that I have given a pretty clear testimony of my faith, and that you will find no more ardent supporter than myself of the divinity of Jesus Christ. My works are in the hands of everyone, and I have at least derived this fruit from them, that my doctrine is approved by all the orthodox churches. Show us, then, the very passage on which you found our accusation of Arianism; for I will wash out this infamy, and will not endure to be unjustly charged."

XI. Labors and Perils in Geneva.

Caroli was overwhelmed by this reply, and appealed to the Council; but they reproved him by ordering him to acknowledge in public the innocence of the ministers he had slandered. To avoid this, he fled to Rome, and was received into the Romish church.

The many gross abuses with regard to morals caused Calvin and Farel to press forward the work of Reformation by an attempt to purge the city.

This was a far more difficult task than they had anticipated. The "Libertines," worldly men who desired to live as they pleased, opposed all measures proposed in the right direction; and at length the city elections gave them a majority. This placed the pastors in a position of grave difficulty; but they stood firm. The difficulty was increased by the fact that the cause of the Reformation was now as much in the hands of the Council as in those of the preachers. This mixing of the church and the state must have been responsible for much of the disorder that followed.

The Council of Berne counselled that of Geneva to restore certain ceremonies; among which was the use of unleavened bread in the Communion. Calvin perceived here his opportunity to protest against the bread and wine being given at all to the Libertines. The question at issue was thus obscured by the action of the Council, who were fighting for the use of unleavened bread, while the Reformers were standing for the purity of the Lord's table.

Easter Sunday, 1538, saw the battle between the opposed parties. Farel in one church, Calvin in another, expounded the nature of the Lord's Supper, describing the necessary qualifications of worthy communicants; and concluding by stating that on that day the Holy Supper would not be dispensed at all. Both the parties were resolute. Calvin declared that his blood should dye the wood he stood upon rather than dishonor his Lord. "We protest before you all that we are not obstinate about the question of bread, leavened or unleavened. That is a matter of indifference, which is felt to the discretion of the church. If we decline to administer the Lord's

Supper, it is because we are in a great difficulty, which prompts us to this course."

This was the occasion of a fierce storm of public disorder and riot. The Council sent for the preachers, and ordered them to leave the city at once. "Well and good; God has done it!" was their sorrowful reply as they withdrew. "Had I been the servant of man," added Calvin, "I should have received but poor wages. But happy for me it is that I am the servant of Him who never fails to give His servants that which He has promised them."

In banishing the two pastors, the Council did what has been done in numerous other cases;—they condemned them on a false issue. They based their sentence upon the charge that the pastors refused their sanction to the use of unleavened bread. But the pastors treated the absence of leaven as a thing indifferent in itself. It was the presence of the leaven of wickedness in the Libertines that drew forth their decision. But they were condemned; and the two banished servants of Christ "departed from the presence of the Council, rejoicing that they were counted worthy to suffer shame" for Christ's sake.

XII. The Doctrines of Grace.

The design of this work has included from the beginning a brief yet prominent place for a view of those holy and glorious truths which are commonly known as the "doctrines of grace."

These views of divine truth are often so connected with the Reformer's name as to be termed "Calvinistic." Not that Calvin was the first to teach them. They are the doctrines, that is, the *teachings,* of the Bible, of the Lord Jesus, of Paul. They are the truths that have ennobled kingdoms, animated martyrs, broken the chains of sin, and opened the gate of life.

They are the truths that have produced rich fruit in life, and given comfort in death to uncounted thousands of believers.

Yet, partly because Calvin was used of God to revive much truth that had been obscured by error, and partly because he taught these doctrines as a system of truth, they have received the designation of Calvinism.

The difference between what is called the Arminian view and that which is known as the Calvinistic may be briefly stated thus. The former teaches that man by nature has both will and power to turn to God, to repent, believe, obey, and do all that the gospel requires. The latter teaches that man by nature has neither will nor power to produce any spiritual desire or act; and that therefore the work of grace is begun, continued, and completed entirely and alone by the sovereign grace of God.

I can never forget being as a child entranced by reading in a book of astronomy how the older astronomers placed the earth in the center, and taught that the sun and the whole universe of stars revolved around this globe. And how the astronomers of a later century placed the sun in the center of our system; and thus brought order out of confusion.

Something like this occurred on an after day when by divine teaching the sweet "doctrines of grace" were revealed in their majesty, and applied in their power.

Let it be realized here that this is not a theological work, either of doctrine or of experience. This brief outline of doctrine is only intended to illustrate the life of Calvin; and this fact must limit both thought and expression.

The doctrines known as Calvinistic are usually stated as *five,* though a larger number might be given. But the usual classification will answer the present purpose; and for the sake of conciseness they will be given in their proper sequence.

1. The *first* of these great truths is *"Original Sin."* By this is meant that, as a result of the Fall of the first Adam, all his descendants are born in a fallen condition, and destitute of spiritual life. That every person, at his first birth, is "dead in trespasses and sins," without will to what is good, and without power to repent and believe.

Original sin consists in apostasy from God, alienation of the will, a darkened condition of the understanding, and a complete infection of the whole being, body and soul. This is abundantly plain from the Word of God, and is made feelingly plain to those who by the Spirit of God are "convinced of sin." We are thus "by nature children of wrath," that is, subject to the wrath of God.

All practical sin is the result of original sin, as the fruit grows upon the tree, as the stream issues from the fountain. This foundation truth is of vital importance. To miss its import is to be liable to every error, and the prey of every "wind of doctrine." Therefore, "marvel not that I said unto thee, ye *must* be born again" (John 3:7).

2. The *second* great truth is the doctrine of *Election.* This word simply means *choice.* By the doctrine is meant the sovereign, free, eternal, unmerited, and unalterable choice on the part of God of persons to everlasting life and salvation. With this doctrine is usually joined that

XII. The Doctrines of Grace.

of *Predestination*, which is the eternal decree of God, determining that certain events shall take place. The word "predestination," as a noun, does not occur in the New Testament; but the verb translated "predestinated" occurs six times (Acts 4:28; Romans 8:29,30; 1 Corinthians 2:7; Ephesians 1:5,11). The English word does not appear at all in the Revised Version.

With this doctrine it is also usual to attach that of *Reprobation*, which is indeed a necessary consequence. By this is meant, when properly understood, the decree of God which justly leaves some persons where their sin has placed them. The Westminster Confession says of this: "The rest of mankind God was pleased, according to the unsearchable counsel of His own will, whereby He extendeth or withholdeth mercy, as He pleaseth, for the glory of His sovereign power over His creatures, to pass by, and to ordain them to dishonor and wrath, *for their sin*, to the praise of His glorious justice."

These twin truths can be abundantly proved from Scripture; and our wisdom is to bow to whatever is taught in that holy treasury of truth. The word translated "election" occurs seven times in the New Testament (Acts 9:15: "a vessel of election unto Me"; Romans 9:11; 11:5, 7, 28; 1 Thessalonians 1:4; 2 Peter 1:10). The adjective translated "elect" or "chosen" occurs twenty-three times in the New Testament. The verb "to elect" or "to choose," that is, on God's part, occurs twenty times. We have therefore *fifty* occurrences of this doctrine in the New Testament.

This truth is hated by the carnal mind of man, and many are the objections raised against it. All of these are very familiar, both by experience and by argument; but every objection vanishes and melts away in the sweet light of God's Word when applied with power. Were this the place for a controversial view of this holy truth, the ground could be taken from under the feet of any objector by one simple argument: If God *can* save all men, and all men are not saved, it follows that the exercise of His power is withheld; and this must logically amount to a sovereign choice of those who are saved.

I have sometimes in ministry asked a question, leaving the answer to the court of the conscience of the hearer: Two dying robbers were crucified with the Lord of life; why was one saved, and not the other? There can ultimately be only one answer to this question.

3. The *third* great truth is known by the expression *"Particular Redemption."* By this is meant that the atonement of Christ is not universal, either in its intention or its application. This naturally follows upon a divine choice of persons; redemption being effected for those who were ordained to eternal life and chosen to salvation.

The objection urged against this truth based upon the word "all" and the word "world" falls at once to the ground upon an examination of the words. The objection raised that this doctrine excludes any from salvation is a very weak one in the mouth of an Arminian, who professes to believe that a redeemed person may be finally lost. Were this the intended place, it could be proved that the Arminian system is illogical and absurd as well as unscriptural.

Redemption is described in Scripture as "precious" (Psalm 49:8), "plenteous" (Psalm 130:7), and "eternal" (Hebrews 9:12). Redemption is the payment of a price for the object bought. The price was the blood of Christ. The object purchased was the "church of God." From redemption flow all new covenant blessings, life, godly sorrow, faith, forgiveness of sin, adoption, love, peace.

4. The *fourth* great truth known as "Calvinistic" is that of *"Effectual Calling."* By this is meant that all who are chosen to life and redeemed by blood shall, at an appointed time, be quickened into life by the Holy Spirit, and be called by grace into the knowledge of the truth.

The word "effectual" is used to distinguish this call from the open, or outward, call of the gospel as it is preached, which is universal wherever it comes. "Unto you, O men, I call; and My voice is to the sons of man" (Proverbs 8:4). "For many are called, but few are chosen" (Matthew 22:14). This outward call in preaching may be *refused* (Proverbs 1:24; Hebrews 12:25), *rejected* (John 12:48), *put away* (Acts 13:46), *neglected* (Hebrews 2:3), and *disobeyed* (1 Peter 4:17). But the "effectual call" is *holy* (2 Timothy 1:9), *almighty* (Romans 1:16), *attracting* (John 12:32), *quickening* (John 5:25), *effective* (1 Thessalonians 1:5), and *irresistible* (Romans 8:27).

5. The *fifth* great "doctrine of grace" is that of the *Final Preservation* of all those who are chosen. By this is meant that, as they have been chosen to salvation by God the Father, redeemed by God the Son, and quickened by God the Holy Spirit, they will receive grace so to endure to the end as that they must infallibly be saved. To reason against this is to question the wisdom, will, love, grace, and even the power of God. It is to charge Him with fickleness of purpose and inability to accomplish that which He intended and began.

Three scriptures occur to the mind in penning the last sentence; and with them this chapter must close. "And this is the Father's will which sent Me, that of all which He hath given Me I should lose nothing, but should raise it up again at the last day" (John 6:39). "And I give unto them eternal life; and they shall never perish, neither shall any man pluck them out of My hand" (John 10:28). "Being confident of this very thing, that He which hath begun a good work in you will perform it until the day of Jesus Christ" (Philippians 1:6).

The objections to these high and holy truths are best met by appeal to the unerring Word. No argument can stand against what is written there. Yet, remembering the haughty malice of *one* heart in days long gone by, what remains but tender compassion for those who now oppose, and a desire for their salvation. Others there are who find these doctrines stones of stumbling in their path, yet sincere, tender, willing to learn: these we love to take by the hand to the Great Infallible Teacher, and leave them with Him in the sweet light of His Written Word.

XIII. Calvin's Work at Strasburg.

Following the command of their Lord, that, when persecuted in one city, they should "flee to another," the two Reformers, Calvin and Farel, retired from Geneva; we cannot doubt with much sadness of heart, and feeling disappointed at the apparent interruption of their work. This was in April, 1538.

They appear to have wandered in Switzerland for about four months. A glimpse of Calvin's feelings at this time is given us by his letter to Louis de Tillet, dated July 10th, 1538: "On looking back, and considering the perplexities which environed me from the time when I first went thither, there is nothing I dread more than returning to the charge from which I have been set free. For while, when first I entered upon it, I could discern the calling of God, which held me fast bound, with which I consoled myself, now, on the contrary, I am in fear lest I tempt Him if I resume so great a burden, which has been already felt to be insupportable.

Nevertheless, I know assuredly that our Lord will guide me in that so very doubtful a deliberation; the more so because I shall look rather to what He will point out to me than to my own judgment, which beyond measure drawing me the contrary way, I feel ought to be suspected."

To his church in Geneva he wrote, October 1st, 1538: "God is our witness, and your own consciences before His judgment-seat, that while we had our conversation among you, our whole study has been to keep you together in happy union and concord....If, avoiding all conflict with men, except only in so far as we are constrained to have them opposed to us, inasmuch as they are the adversaries of Jesus Christ, we do resist the wiles of our spiritual enemy, being furnished with the armor wherewith the Lord would have His people to be girded and strengthened; there need be no fear about our victory. Wherefore, my brethren, if you seek true victory, do not oppose evil by evil of a like kind; but, laying aside all evil affections, be guided solely by your zeal for the service of God, moderated by His Spirit, and ruled by His Word." Golden advice!

Farel went to Neuchatel, which became the scene of his labor to the end of his life. Calvin went to Basle. Staying for a short time in this city, so dear to him, he received an invitation from Bucer and Capito, the Protestant pastors of Strasburg, to settle with them there. To this request he acceded, yet not without hesitation. In August he wrote to Farel: "I suspect that Bucer will press me more strongly to go to Strasburg. I shall not fall in with this unless I am compelled by a greater necessity." In his Preface to the Psalms he writes: "Being at liberty and released from my office, I had thought of living in peace, until Martin Bucer, using a remonstrance and protestation like those which Farel had used before, recalled me to another place."

This city had become the refuge of thousands of persecuted persons, chiefly from France; and, attracted by Calvin's preaching, many flocked there from other places. A large congregation of these refugees made him their pastor. He reached Strasburg in September, 1538, and remained there exactly three years.

In his new sphere of labor, the Town Council appointed him to give lectures on Scripture. Here he lectured every day to the students, taking the Gospel by John and the Epistle to the Romans as the basis of his expositions. In addition to this, he preached in the Dominican church four times a week, besides being engaged in his pastoral duties. These lectures drew students from other countries, so that Strasburg promised to become a rival to Wittenberg as a center of gospel light.

It appears that Calvin at this time was suffering from

extreme poverty, as he wrote to Farel to say that he "did not possess a farthing." The senate afterwards appointed him a small stipend.

But what was the condition in Geneva after the departure of Farel and Calvin? With an eye ever alert, the papacy saw a grand opportunity, in the absence of the Reformers, and in the presence of much disorder following their removal, to obtain a victory there. Accordingly, an able Romanist, Cardinal Sadoleto, was appointed by the pope to write a letter "to the Senate and People of Geneva." This letter was as craftily worded as if it had been penned by a fox. In elegant language (Latin) the writer coined some glowing sentences in praise of Scripture, of salvation by Christ, and of justification by faith. But interwoven with all this was his sincere lament that the Genevese had forsaken the true fold, the papacy.

The effect of this remarkable epistle was not at all what the author, or his papal master, anticipated. It rather operated to alarm the people of Geneva, and certainly helped them to perceive the great folly of their recent acts, and the danger thereby produced.

Whilst this condition of anxiety existed at Geneva, Calvin obtained at Strasburg a copy of the cardinal's letter, and immediately set to work to write a reply. It occupied him for six days, and as a piece of reasoning and of literature, it is worthy of the pen that wrote it.

This masterly reply took up the compliments and the arguments of the cardinal's letter, and answered them one by one. An extract must suffice here: "The men of Geneva, extricating themselves from the slough of error in which they were sunk, have returned to the doctrine of the gospel; and this you call abandoning the truth of God. They have withdrawn from papal tyranny; and this you say is to separate from the church."

Calvin's reply speedily spread far and wide. Copies were sent to Wittenberg, and Luther obtained one. "Here," said the German Reformer, "is a writing which has hands and feet. I rejoice that God raises up such men. They will continue what I have begun against Antichrist, and by the help of God they will complete it."

XIII. Calvin's Work at Strasburg.

We must not fail to realize here that Calvin's other writings had reached Luther, notably his great work, the *Institutes*. Luther's writings also were being circulated all over Europe. The question arises, and it is a very natural one: Did Luther and Calvin ever meet?

The answer has its touching aspect. They did not. According to human judgment, immense good would have occurred from a meeting of these two great Reformers. Luther's bold, aggressive, fearless, impetuous, Teutonic zeal; Calvin gentle, majestic, refined, yet commanding learning. We should have thought that the effect of contact would be beneficial to each, and that each would receive something of advantage from the other. But we must never overlook that each did his own work better than the other could have done it; and that Christ knew the suitable sphere for the impetuous Peter and for the loving John. In one of his letters to Luther, Calvin says: "Oh, if I could fly towards thee, and enjoy thy society, if only for a few hours!" We can almost imagine, moreover, that the influence of Calvin upon Luther in the controversy about the Lord's Supper would have healed the breach between Germany and Geneva, and would have convinced Luther of his mistake in refusing to concede one easily-said word in response to Zwingli and others.

But, alas! God's workmen have their blemishes. Each light-bearing pitcher is an *earthen* vessel, that the excellency of the power may be of God and not of them.

Moreover, we observe a similar disposition in the works of creation.

Saturn could not move in the orbit of Jupiter; nor could Venus glitter in our morning or evening sky in any orbit but her own. The oak, the ash, the elm, are clothed in the beauty most suited to each. And most certainly Calvin molded and continued and strengthened what Luther had begun.

We are able to record that Calvin the scholar and Melancthon the theologian met at this time. The concessions which Melancthon had proposed at times in his loving desire for peace had not the full approval of Calvin; but he never doubted the loyalty of Melancthon to the cause of God and truth. It is possible that Melancthon somewhat leaned to Luther's view of the Lord's Supper; yet with the full knowledge of this, Calvin, in his letters to Farel, expressed his delight in Melancthon. *And this was as it should be now.* Why should a slight difference on a minor point be magnified into a fatal error when a servant of Christ is sound to the core by Divine teaching on all essential truth? It is certain that the friendship of Calvin and Melancthon was real, and that it continued throughout their lives, to the great advantage of the church of God.

How deep, and pure, and touching the love of Calvin towards Melancthon was will be seen in the following, written by the former after the death of the latter: "O Philip Melancthon—for it is thou whom, I address— thou who now livest at the hand of God with Christ, awaiting us on high till we are gathered with thee into blessed repose, a hundred times hast thou said to me when, wearied with toil and vexation, thou didst lean thy head upon my bosom, Would to God, would to God, that I might die upon that bosom! As for me, later, a hundred times have I wished that it had been granted us to be together. Certainly thou wouldst have been bolder to face struggles, more courageous to despise envy and calumny. Then also would have been suppressed the malignity of many whose audacity increased in proportion to what they called thy weak-minded fear."

While Calvin was at Strasburg, a further attempt was made by the papacy to check the Reformation, this time by appearing to make concessions. A conference was begun at Hagenau, on June 25th, 1540, and adjourned to the 28th. Calvin was deputed to be present. On June 30th the conference was again adjourned. It was summoned to meet at Ratisbon in January, 1541, but did not open until April. Calvin's keen mind perceived some insincerity in those who called this meeting, and his expectations of real gospel fruit were not great. Yet during the early days much was discussed, and some concessions were made by the Romanists. But when the question of

XIII. Calvin's Work at Strasburg.

the Real Presence came up for discussion, Calvin found it impossible to concede one hair's breadth. Things indifferent he yielded; but truth on this point he felt must be maintained at all cost. "There," he said, "stood the impassable rock which barred the way to further progress. I had to explain in Latin what were my sentiments. Without fear of offense I condemned that peculiar *local* presence. The act of adoration I declared to be altogether insufferable."

The conference ended without any real and substantial fruit. Light and darkness, truth and error, sweet and bitter, had met; but they could not coalesce. The design of Rome had been to *absorb* the Reformation, which would have been equivalent to devouring it. But the design had failed; and henceforth the Reformation and the papacy turned each to its own path.

Would to God that the similar attempt on the part of Rome today to *absorb* our beloved country might have the same result!

It was while an exile at Strasburg that Calvin married, at the age of 31. His choice was Idelette de Bure, the widow of a Belgian refugee, Jean Storder.

She is described as being an eminently suitable partner in every way, a true helper, with true sympathy. "A most choice woman," writes Beza.

His married life lasted only nine years. They had only one child, who lived but a few days. His wife died in March, 1549.

Of her, Calvin writes to Peter Viret, after her death: "My sorrow is no common one. I have lost the excellent companion of my life, who, if misfortune had come upon us, would have gladly shared with me, not merely exile and wretchedness, but death itself. While she lived, she was the faithful helper of my ministry; and never did I experience from her the least hindrance."

XIV. The Reformer's Work at Geneva.

The Ratisbon Conference having been so unsuccessful, and the disorders at Geneva so continuous since the expulsion of the two Reformers, that city began to think that it might be desirable to recall them. Accordingly, three attempts were made to induce Calvin to return; but he hesitated.

Then private letters were written to him by the citizens, begging him to return.

In his reply to the Council he wrote, October 23rd, 1540: "I am in singular perplexity; having the desire to meet your wish, and to wrestle with all the grace that God has given me to get her brought back into a better condition.

"On the other hand, I cannot slightingly quit, or lay down lightly, the charge to which the Lord has called me, without being relieved of it by regular and lawful means. For so have I always believed and taught, and to the present moment cannot persuade myself to the contrary, that when our Lord appoints a man as pastor in a church to teach in His Word, he ought to consider himself as engaged to take the government of it, so that he may not lightly withdraw from it, or without the settled testimony in his own heart, and the testimony of the faithful, that the Lord has discharged him."

To Viret he wrote: "I could not read one part of your letter without a laugh. It is that in which you exhibit so much care for my prosperity. Shall I then go to Geneva to secure my peace? Why not rather submit to be crucified? It would be better to perish at once than to be tormented to death in that chamber of torture. If you wish indeed my welfare, dear Viret, pray cease from such advice as this."

To Farel he wrote: "Who will not pardon me, if I do not again willingly throw myself into a whirlpool which I have found so dangerous?"

At length Bucer urged upon him that it was his duty to return; and this argument was one likely to prevail with him. It did prevail. Then, in May, 1541, the Council of Geneva revoked the sentence of exile pronounced against the Reformers in 1538.

On September 13th, 1541, Calvin returned to Geneva, and took up the work which had been interrupted. The Council provided him a house, and voted him a stipend of 500 florins per year, equal to £140. The Reformer lost no time in entering upon his work. Within a few days of his arrival, the citizens were summoned to the cathedral for confession of sin and prayer to God. After this, Calvin set himself to construct for Geneva a form of government that would establish the Reformation on a secure basis. His idea seems to have been a kind of Biblical Republic combining church and state into one organization, very much after the order of things prevailing in the time of Moses. It is important to realize this, as it will explain much of what followed. Writing to Farel on September 16th, 1541, he says of this: "Immediately after I had offered my services to the Senate, I declared that a church could not hold together unless a settled government should be agreed on, such as is prescribed to us in the Word of God, and such as was in use in the ancient church. I requested that they would appoint certain of their number who might confer with us on the subject. Six were then appointed."

A draft of the agreed laws of discipline was presented to the Council on September 28th; and its history then is: examination continued to October 27; adopted by the Two Hundred, November 9; accepted by the General Council, November 20; and finally voted by the people on January 2nd, 1542. "It is from that date," records Bungener, "that the Calvinistic republic legally dates."

The church was to be governed by four orders: pastors, doctors, elders, deacons. The pastors were to rule, the doctors to teach, the elders to govern, and the deacons to receive and pay money.

This authority was vested in a "Consistory," which was composed of six ministers and twelve elders. The elders were elected annually, and were to be men of good and blameless conduct moved by the fear of God. They were required to take the oath of allegiance to the state and of fidelity to the church. They therefore represented the idea that Geneva was a *Church-State*. This was Calvin's high ideal. Their duty was to look after the conduct of every citizen; and their power was to punish every breach of the rules of the state. Its jurisdiction therefore was not only civil, but spiritual. Every church question thus tended to become civil; and every civil question to become ecclesiastical. It was not recognized by Geneva that the two would never unite, so long as human nature remains what it is. This arrangement afterwards caused confusion and resistance.

The Consistory sat every Thursday to examine charges of misconduct, to administer justice, to punish offenders. Every offense against the church, such as refusal to attend divine service, and especially "heresy," thus became a civil offense, punishable by the city magistrates.

These principles of "church-and-state" government were not solely Calvin's: they were shared by all the pastors at Zurich, Berne, Basle, and Geneva alike. In these ideas they were neither before nor behind their age: but the one thing that has laid Calvin more open to attack is the fact that he defended his position with calm and logical argument. His great fault, if fault it was, was his idea, which, however, he only shared with other Reformers, of building up a spiritual church upon the sandy foundation of an earthly republic; or at least of welding the two into one.

If it be objected that this was an impossible attempt to rule a city, it may be answered that it was fully voted by the entire population. The condition could only continue so long as the majority wished it. "The more

XIV. The Reformer's Work at Geneva.

this legislation has been studied," writes Bungener, "the more is it seen to be in advance of all previous systems of legislation. The form sometimes surprises us a little by its quaint simplicity, but the grandeur of the whole is not the less evident to those who seek it. This was about to manifest itself in the history of the humble nation to whom this legislation was to give so glorious a place in the intellectual as well as in the religious world."

The labors of Calvin at this time were great and manifold. In addition to the work of each Lord's day, he preached on each day of every alternate week. Every week were three expository lectures. Every Thursday he preached in the university, and every Friday gave a public exposition.

When the plague broke out, he gave his services freely in visiting the sick and dying. His correspondence from every country was immense; nor did he withhold help from any, far or near, who needed what was in his power to give. And there is one marvelous feature about his writings, whether his books or his ordinary letters,— that though they are so numerous, there is not an immature sentence in them all. Every word has its own native depth and ripeness, and is full of real *teaching*.

But we have now to trace the rise and continuance of events that were full of bitter strife and sorrow. Galled by the strictness of the city discipline, and rebelling against all constituted authority, a party of men named "Libertines" was formed. These gave much trouble and concern by reason of the disorder they produced. One day, says Bungener, "in the large hall of the cloisters, behind the cathedral, Calvin was giving his usual divinity lecture. Around his chair hundreds were thronging, and amongst them numbers of future preachers and martyrs. Suddenly they heard outside laughter, cries, and a great clamor. It proceeded from fifteen or twenty Libertines, who, out of hatred to Calvin and his teaching, were giving a specimen of their manners, and of what they called liberty."

The battle between Geneva and the Libertines lasted nine years. This would not be the place to even hint at the vile immoralities practiced by these deluded people, of both sexes, as the natural fruit of their sentiments. Setting aside all laws, human and divine, they became a law to themselves. One of them, Pierre Ameaux, a maker of playing-cards, was a member of the Two Hundred. His wife was arrested for immoral practices, and imprisoned. He then spoke against the pastors, and was compelled to make a public apology. This was the signal for a general revolt on the part of the Libertines.

In 1547, one of their number, in heart a papist, Jacques Gruet, fixed a paper on the pulpit of St. Peter's, full of scurrilous abuse of the ministers, with threats of violence and death. Moreover, he was adjudged to be guilty of treachery to the state, and of blasphemy. He received the sentence of death.

In December, 1547, the Two Hundred met to discuss the position, and the contention rose so high that the pastors, especially Calvin, were in danger of their lives. In this midst of this tumult, Calvin addressed the Council: "I know that I am the primary cause of these divisions and disturbances. If it is my life you desire, I am ready to die. If it is my banishment you wish, I shall exile myself. If you desire once more to save Geneva without the Gospel, you can try."

This challenge produced a sobering effect upon the Council, as it recalled to their minds the former exile of their pastor, and its results. The storm subsided, but only to break out again more fiercely. The Reformer was openly insulted in the streets; dogs were called by his name; and his name was pronounced as if spelt "Cain."

It was at this dark hour that his wife was called away from him by death.

Her last words were: "O glorious resurrection! God of Abraham and of all our fathers, not one of the faithful who have hoped in Thee, for so many ages, has been disappointed. I also will hope."

We now approach the darkest hour of Geneva. While the Libertines were asserting themselves against all authority, in 1552, a physician named Servetus, who has already been introduced to us in chapter vii, who

XIV. The Reformer's Work at Geneva.

had been condemned to death at Vienne, fled to Geneva. The Libertines saw in him the very person they desired to oppose to the Reformer; and the two made common cause against him. Servetus was arrested and imprisoned; how and why is reserved for a chapter to itself, on account of its great importance as affecting Calvin.

Two men, Perrin and Berthelier, had been debarred from the Lord's table by the Consistory on account of their evil lives. The latter demanded that his sentence should be annulled; and in the face of a remonstrance from Calvin his demand was granted. Everything therefore now seemed to be against the Reformer and the Reformation.

The following Lord's day, September 3rd, was the day appointed for the celebration of the communion; and Calvin, seeing the danger, assembled all the pastors, and proceeded with them to the General Council. With one consent the pastors promised to stand firm to oppose the desecration of the Lord's table. The council were not to be moved. The Libertines now appeared to be in view of a great victory.

The eventful morning dawned. The bell invited the people to the church of St. Peter. The Libertines were present, with their swords, determined to communicate. Calvin preached on the intention of the sacred ordinance, and spoke of the state of mind necessary for obedience to the Lord's command. At the close, he said: "As for me, so long as God shall leave me here, since He hath given me fortitude, and I have received it from Him, I will employ it, whatever betide; and I will guide myself by my Master's rule, which to me is clear and well known. As we are now about to receive the holy Supper of our Lord Jesus Christ, if anyone who has been debarred by the Consistory shall approach this table, *though it should cost my life,* I will show myself such as I ought to be."

He then left the pulpit, and stood at the table. Removing the white cloth, and covering the bread and wine with his hands, he said, with a voice that rang through the building, *"These hands you may crush; these arms you may lop off; my life you may take; my blood is yours, you may shed it but you shall never force me to give holy things to the profane, and dishonor the table of my God."* As if the very power of God prevailed, a calm succeeded, and the Libertines retired; the congregation opening a passage for their retreat. A solemn silence enabled the Reformer to celebrate the sacred ordinance in awe, as if the Lord Himself had been manifestly present.

The question in the mind of Calvin was not whether he or the Libertines should succeed; but whether the Reformation should be wrecked at the very table of the Lord. He stood firm; and victory remained with him.

On the evening of the same day Calvin preached again in the same pulpit.

He chose for his subject the farewell words of Paul to the elders of the church of Ephesus (Acts 20:1). In the full belief that he was preaching his farewell sermon, he spread forth his hands, and "commended them to God and to the word of His grace," amid the sobs and tears of all present.

But no sentence of banishment came to him. He was left undisturbed by the Council; for the counsels of men are subject to a Higher power than their own.

The Late Mr. Spurgeon's Visit to Geneva.

An account of the late Mr. C. H. Spurgeon's visit to the town of Calvin, which he gave in the course of his address at the first meeting held in the Metropolitan Tabernacle, August 21st, 1860, is so interesting, and so in harmony with this narrative, that we must make room for it here.

"At last we came to Geneva. I had received the kindest invitation from our esteemed and excellent brother, Dr. D'Aubigne. He came to meet me at the station, but he missed me. I met a gentleman in the street, and told him I was Mr. Spurgeon. He then said, 'Come to my house, — the very house where Calvin used to live.' I went home with him; and after we found Dr. D'Aubigne and Pastor Bard, I was taken to the house of Mr. Lombard, an eminent banker of the city, and a godly and gracious man. I think I never enjoyed a time more than I did with those real true-hearted brethren. There are, you know, two churches there,—the Established and the Free; and there has been some little jealousy, but I think it is all dying away. At any rate, I saw little of it, for brethren from both these churches came, and showed me every kindness and honor. I am not superstitious, but the first time I saw this medal, bearing the venerated likeness of John Calvin, I kissed it, imagining that no one saw the action. I was very greatly surprised when I received this magnificent present, which shall be passed round for your inspection. On the one side is John Calvin with his visage worn by disease and deep thought; and on the other side is a verse fully applicable to him: 'He endured, as seeing Him who is invisible.'

"This sentence truly describes the character of that glorious man of God. Among all those who have been born of women, there has not risen a greater than John Calvin. No age before him ever produced his equal, and no age afterwards has seen his rival. In theology, he stands alone, shining like a bright fixed star, while other leaders and teachers can only circle round him, at a great distance, with nothing like his glory or his permanence. Calvin's fame is eternal because of the truth he proclaimed; and even in heaven, although we shall lose the name of the system of doctrine which he taught, it shall be that truth which shall make us strike our golden harps, and sing: 'Unto Him that loved us, and washed us from our sins in His own blood, and hath made us kings and priests unto God and His Father; to Him be glory for ever and ever.' For the essence of Calvinism is that we are born again, 'not of blood, nor of the will of the flesh, nor of the will of man, but of God.'

"I preached in the cathedral of Geneva; and I thought it a great honor to be allowed to stand in the pulpit of John Calvin. I do not think half the people understood me; but they were very glad to see and join *in heart* with the worship in which they could not join with the understanding. I did not feel very happy when I came out in full canonicals; but the request was put to me in such a beautiful form that I could have worn the pope's tiara, if by so doing I could have preached the gospel the more freely. They said, 'Our dear brother comes to us from another country. Now, when an ambassador comes from another land, he has the right to wear his own costume at court; but, as a mark of great esteem, he sometimes condescends to the manners of the people he is visiting, and wears their court dress.' 'Well,' I said, 'yes, that I will, certainly, if you do not require it, but merely ask it as a token of my Christian love. I shall feel like running in a sack, but it will be your fault.' It was John Calvin's gown, and that reconciled me to it very much. I do love that man of God; suffering all his life long, enduring not only persecutions from without, but a complication of disorders from within, and yet serving his Master with all his heart.

"After the service in the Cathedral, it was arranged for me to meet the ministers. D'Aubigne was there, of course, and Caesar Malan, and most of the noted preachers of Switzerland. We spent a very delightful evening together, talking about our common Lord, and of the progress of His work in England and on the Continent.

"It was a peculiar pleasure to me to have the opportunity of visiting that great center of earnest Protestantism, and of meeting so many of the godly and faithful men who had helped to keep the lamp of truth burning brightly. To my dying day I shall remember those servants of Jesus Christ who greeted me in my Master's Name, and loved me for my Master's sake."

XV. Calvin and Servetus.

A calm and impartial view of this sad subject has been reserved for this place, and for a chapter of its own. The immense advantage of having been able to consult and to weigh the evidence of the principal writers—certainly not fewer than forty—about the case of Servetus, besides several biographies of the man himself, will greatly aid the writer.

It is very common to hear the remark, "What about Servetus?" or, "Who burned Servetus?"

There are three kinds of persons who thus flippantly ask a question of this nature. First, the Roman Catholics, who may judge it to be an unanswerable taunt to a Protestant. Second, those who are not in accord with the great doctrines of grace, as taught by Paul and Calvin, and embraced and loved by thousands still. Then there is a third kind of persons who can only be described as ill-informed. It is always desirable, and often useful, to really know something of what one professes to know.

I shall narrow the enquiry at the outset by saying that all Roman Catholics are "out of court." They burn heretics on principle, avowedly. This is openly taught by them; it is in the margin of their Bible; and it is even their boast that they do so. And, moreover, they condemned Servetus to be burned.

Those who misunderstand or misrepresent the doctrines of grace call for pity more than blame when they charge the death of Servetus upon those views of divine truth known as Calvinistic. Perhaps a little instruction would be of great value to such. It is very desirable to have clear ideas of what it is we are trying to understand. In most disputes this would make a clear pathway for thought and argument. Most controversies are more about terms than principles.

The third sort of persons are plainly incompetent to take up this case, for the simple reason that they know nothing whatever about it. Pressed for their reasons, they have to confess that they never at any time read a line about the matter.

The duty of the historian is not to plead, but to narrate facts. I shall do this as impartially as possible. One writer need not be imitated (W. H. Drummond, D.D.), who is not ashamed to disfigure his title-page: "Life of Michael Servetus, who was entrapped, imprisoned, and burned by John Calvin." Less scurrilous, but equally prejudiced, is Dr. R. Willis. It is a weak case that needs the aid of ink mixed with abusive gall.

The simplest method of arranging my material will be to ask and to answer three questions. First, *why* was Servetus burned? Second, *who* burned him? Third, *what part* in the matter was taken by John Calvin?

Michael Servetus was born at Villanueva, in 1509. After a liberal education, he studied medicine; and anticipated Harvey in the discovery of the circulation of the blood. It appears that he had a lively genius, but was unstable, erratic, and weak.

In 1530 he published a book "On the Errors of the Trinity." His views need not be given here; one specimen will suffice to give an idea of them. He said that the doctrine of the Trinity was "a three-headed Cerberus, a dream of Augustine, and an invention of the devil."

The book, however, on which his trial was based was his *"Restitutio Christianismi."* Only two copies of this are known to exist; and both are out of England. I have seen a copy of the reprint of 1790. Servetus sent the manuscript of this to Calvin for his perusal; and a lengthy correspondence took place between them, extending from 1546 to 1548. Of this Calvin says: "When he was at Lyons he sent me three questions to answer. He thought to entrap me. That my answer did not satisfy him I am not surprised." To Servetus himself he wrote: "I neither hate you nor despise you; nor do I wish to persecute you; but I would be as hard as iron when I behold you insulting

XV. CALVIN AND SERVETUS.

sound doctrine with so great audacity."

And now occurs what foundation there is on which is built the accusation against Calvin. It occurs in his well-known letter to Farel, dated February 13th, 1546. "Servetus wrote to me a short time ago, and sent a huge volume of his dreamings and pompous triflings with his letter. I was to find among them wonderful things, and such as I had never before seen; and if I wished, he would himself come. But I am by no means inclined to be responsible for him; and if he come, I will never allow him, supposing my influence worth anything, to depart alive."

There lived at Geneva at this time a Frenchman of Lyons named William Trie; and he had a relative at Lyons named Arneys, a Roman Catholic. After the publication of this book by Servetus, Trie wrote to his friend Arneys a letter in which he said that it was base for Protestants to be burned who really believed in Christ, while such a man as Servetus should be permitted to live to publish his vile errors.

Arneys placed this letter before the Inquisition at Lyons, and cardinal Tournon arrested Servetus at once. Without giving the mass of details, it will be sufficient to say that Servetus escaped from prison one night by a pretext. His trial, however, proceeded in his absence; and on June 17th, 1552, *the sentence of death, namely, "to be burned alive, at a slow fire, till his body be reduced to a cinder," was passed upon him by the Inquisition.* On the same day, his effigy was burned, with five bales of his books.

After wandering for a time, he suddenly turned up in Geneva in July; and was arrested by the Council, which, as we have seen, was at this time opposed to Calvin. What Calvin desired from Servetus was his recantation: "Would that we could have obtained a retractation from Servetus, as we did from Gentilis!"

The thirty-eight articles of accusation were drawn up by Calvin. Two examinations took place. At the second of these, Servetus persisted in one of his errors, namely, that all things, "even this footstool," are the substance of God.

After further examinations, these articles, with the replies of the accused man, were sent to the churches of Zurich, Berne, Basle, and Schaffhausen, with a request for their opinion. Farel's reply is worthy of record: "It will be a wonder if that man, suffering death, should at the time turn to the Lord, dying only one death, whereas he has deserved to die a thousand times."

In another letter, written from Neuchatel, September 8th, 1553, Farel says: "Your desire to mitigate the rigor of punishment is the service of a friend to one who is your mortal enemy. But I beseech you so to act as that no one shall hereafter seek with impunity to publish novel doctrines, and to embroil us all as Servetus has done."

All these circumstances prove that his trial was lengthy, deliberate, and careful; and quite in harmony with the requirements of the age. All the Reformers who were consulted approved of the sentence that was pronounced.

At the last stage of the trial, the discussion lasted for three days. The "lesser Council" were unanimous; and the majority of the Great Council were in favor of capital punishment, and so decided on the last day.

Sentence of death by fire was given on October 26th, to be carried into effect on the following day.

And now one man alone stands forth to plead for a mitigation of the sentence, namely, that another form of death be substituted for the stake. *That one man was John Calvin.* He interceded most earnestly with the judges for this, but in vain.

Both Farel, who came to Geneva for the purpose, and Calvin, prayed with the unhappy man, and expressed themselves tenderly towards him. Both of them pleaded with the Council for the substitution of a milder mode of death; but the syndics were inflexible.

The historian Paul Henry writes of this matter: "Calvin here appears in his real character; and a nearer consideration of the proceeding, examined from the point of view furnished by the age in which he lived, will completely exonerate him from all blame. *His conduct was not determined by personal feeling;* it was the conse-

XV. Calvin and Servetus.

quence of a struggle which this great man had carried on for years against tendencies to a corruption of doctrine which threatened the church with ruin. Every age must be judged according to its prevailing laws; and Calvin cannot be fairly accused of any greater offense than that with which we may be charged for punishing certain crimes with death."

The main facts therefore may now be summarized thus: 1. That Servetus was guilty of blasphemy, of a kind and degree which is still punishable here in England by imprisonment. 2. That his sentence was in accordance with the spirit of the age. 3. That he had been sentenced to the same punishment by the Inquisition at Vienne. 4. That the sentence was pronounced by the Councils of Geneva, Calvin having no power either to condemn or to save him. 5. That Calvin and others visited the unhappy man in his last hours, treated him with much kindness, and did all they could to have the sentence mitigated.

Three hundred and fifty years after the death of Servetus, a "monument of expiation" was erected on the spot where he suffered death at Champel, near Geneva. It bears the date of October 27th, 1903; but the unveiling ceremony was postponed until November 1st.

On one side of this monument are recorded the birth and death of Servetus.

On the front is this inscription: "Dutiful and grateful followers of Calvin our great Reformer, yet condemning an error which was that of his age, and strongly attached to liberty of conscience, according to the true principles of the Reformation and of the Gospel, we have erected this expiatory monument. October 27th, 1903."

Should the Roman Catholic Church desire to follow this example, and erect "monuments of expiation," let her first build one in Paris, and unveil it on August 24th. And doubtless sites would gladly be given for the same purpose in Oxford, Coventry, Maidstone, Lewes, and other places in England. And should Romanists desire the alteration or abrogation of any oath, instead of tampering with the Coronation Oath of Great Britain, let them first annul the oath taken by every bishop at his consecration that he will pursue heretics to the death. All persecution on account of religion and conscience is a violation of the spirit of the gospel, and repugnant to the principles of true liberty.

XVI. Influence upon England.

It would be difficult to estimate the value or measure the extent of the influence of the work and the teaching of John Calvin upon all the countries in Europe that had been visited by the Reformation. Naturally, France and Holland, and next Germany, would be the foremost to fall under that influence; but its vital power and fertilizing warmth were very fruitful in England and Scotland.

Thus Toplady quotes a sentence from Turretin: "John Calvin was a man whose memory will be blessed in every succeeding age. He instructed and enlightened, not only the church of Geneva, but also the whole Reformed world, by his immense labors; insomuch that all the Reformed churches are not seldom called by his name."

It was very natural that a man with his talents should be looked upon as one of the principal Reformers; and that Geneva should be recognized as the center of the work. "He bore," says Beza, "all these churches upon his shoulders." Not only refugees who fled from persecution came to Geneva, but godly pastors from many cities came to see the work of God for themselves.

The "Catechism of Christian Doctrine" was dedicated by its author to the Protestant churches of Austria. In 1549 he dedicated his Commentary on Hebrews to the emperor of Poland, Sigismund Augustus. In 1552 he dedicated the first part of his Commentary on the Acts of the Apostles to Christian I, king of Denmark and Sweden; and the second part, two years later, to his son, Frederick.

As his Commentaries issued from the press, he dedicated them to either exalted persons or to the friends of his youth.

A constant stream of correspondence flowed from Calvin's pen to the Reformers of England. Upon the death of Henry VIII, in 1547, the Duke of Somerset was appointed Protector until Edward VI should come of age.

Somerset earnestly desired the reformation of the Church of England; and this work was largely assisted by the letters from Geneva.

Edward was ten years of age at the death of his father. His talents, and above all, the grace of God which shone so brightly in him, excited the highest hopes of Calvin in regard to him and to England. In June, 1548, Calvin dedicated his Commentary on 1 Timothy to the Protector; and in October of that year he wrote the well-known letter in which he minutely details what was his mind with regard to completing the reformation which had been so well begun in England. "The people should be so taught as to be touched to the quick, and feel that the Word of God is a two-edged sword. I speak this, monseigneur, because it appears to me that there is very little preaching of a lively kind in the kingdom, but that the greater part deliver it by way of reading from a written discourse. This preaching ought not to be lifeless, but lively. Now you know, my lord, how Paul speaks of the liveliness which ought to be in the mouth of good ministers of God, who ought not to make a parade of rhetoric in order to show themselves off, but the Spirit of God must resound in their voice."

The silver trumpet of the pure gospel, and a clear and certain sound in blowing that trumpet, were what Calvin urged upon the attention of the Protector.

There are several letters on record that were addressed to England's Josiah, Edward the Sixth. When this promising young king was fourteen years of age, in January, 1551, Calvin sent the pastor Nicolas des Gallars to England, bearing copies of his Commentaries on Isaiah and the General Epistles. With the books, a letter was addressed to Edward, which is so honorable alike to the writer and to the royal receiver, and also so deserving of our attention today, that a few of its sentences must be inserted here.

> Moreover, Sire, holding myself assured that my letter will have such a reception from you as I desire, I shall not hesitate to pray and beseech you, in the name of Him to whom you ascribe all authority and power, to take courage in following out what you have so well and happily begun, as well in your own person as in the state of your kingdom—namely, the consecration of all to God and to our blessed Savior, who has so dearly purchased us. For, as regards general Reformation, it is not yet so well established as that it should be wise to look on it as achieved. And, in fact, it would be very difficult to purge in a day such an abyss of superstition as there is in the Papacy. Its root is too deep, and has expanded itself too widely, to get so soon to the bottom of it. But, whatever difficulties or delays there may be, the excellence of the work is well worthy of unwearying pursuit.
>
> I have no doubt, Sire, but Satan will put many hindrances in the way before you to slacken your pace, and to make your zeal grow cold. Your subjects, for the most part, do not know the blessing which you procure for them. The great, who are raised to honor, are sometimes too wise in their own conceits to make much account of such work, far less to look to God at all. New and unexpected conflicts arise daily. Now I hope, indeed, Sire, that God has stored you with such greatness and constancy of mind that you will neither be weakened nor wearied by all that; but the thing itself is of so great importance that it well deserves that one should apply to it far more than human strength and energy. Then, after all, when we shall have striven to the very uttermost, there will always remain more waiting to be done.
>
> Meanwhile, Sire, all honest hearts praise God and feel themselves greatly obliged to you that it has pleased you of your favor to grant churches to your subjects who use the French and German languages. In so far as regards the use of the sacraments and spiritual order, I hope that the permission which you have been pleased to confer upon them will bear

fruit.

Howbeit, Sire, I cannot help beseeching once more, feeling so deeply how needful it is, not only that you would secure the rest and contentment of the godly who desire to serve God and to live peacefully in obedience to you, but also that you would restrain vagabond and dissolute people, should such withdraw into your kingdom. I know well, Sire, that you have people of distinguished learning at hand, who can make known to you these things by word of mouth far better than myself by writing; also, that in your council you have men of prudence and zeal to suggest all that is expedient. Among the others, I have no doubt that Monsieur the Duke of Somerset spares no trouble to follow out that wherein he has employed himself so faithfully hitherto. But I believe, Sire, that all that shall be no hindrance to prevent your kind reception of what you will recognize as proceeding from a like source.

To conclude, Sire. Forasmuch as I fear to have already wearied you with my tediousness, I pray you in respect of that, as in everything else, that you would please excuse and pardon me of your kind favor, to which very humbly I beg to be commended, having besought our gracious God and Father to maintain and uphold you in His holy protection, to guide you by His Spirit, and to cause His name to be more and more glorified by you.

John Calvin.
Geneva, January, 1551.

Many of his letters were also addressed to Thomas Cranmer, archbishop, reformer, and afterwards martyr. In one of his epistles to Geneva, Cranmer proposed that godly men, well taught in the school of Christ, and able to teach others, should unite to set forth a common Confession of Christian doctrine. To this proposal Calvin replied: "As far as I am concerned, I will readily pass over ten seas to effect the object in view. If the welfare of England alone were concerned, I should think it a sufficient reason to act thus. But at present, when our purpose is to unite the sentiments of all good and learned men, and so, according to the rule of Scripture, to bring the separated churches into one, neither labor nor trouble of any kind ought to be spared."

This was indeed a laudable desire, and prompted by kindly feelings towards England. But the early death of Edward, and the martyrdom of Cranmer, prevented the fulfillment of the desire. And then the black and fiery reign of Mary did all it could to restore the papacy.

But God had mercy on England, and shortened the days of persecution.

The accession of Elizabeth was like the rising of the sun after a black night of tempest, to the great joy of the godly both here and in Switzerland.

Perceiving his opportunity, Calvin re-opened his correspondence, and dedicated another of his Commentaries to the new queen. He wrote to her, urging that the faith of the gospel, taught and followed by Wycliffe, Tyndale, and Cranmer, might be revived and encouraged by her bishops; and that the goodly church order set up by Cranmer, but interrupted by the fires, might be restored.

The author of the immortal *Rock of Ages,* Augustus Montague Toplady, conclusively proves that the Reformers and martyrs of England, and the translators of our Bible, were Calvinistic; and that the Church of England herself is Calvinistic. Her Articles and Homilies are clearly modeled after the doctrines of grace. In fact, it was not until the days of Laud, at the opening of the seventeenth century, that Arminian teaching began to prevail to any great extent in England. All this is most ably and lucidly presented by Toplady in his "Historic Proof of the Doctrinal Calvinism of the Church of England," in the second volume of his works (6 volumes, 1825). This able and impartial writer shows conclusively, quoting a large number of authors to prove his point, that the Church of England, her bishops, her Articles, her Universities, her martyrs, loyally held those views of Divine truth commonly called Calvinistic, until the defection introduced by Laud.

The Romanist writer, Stapleton, confirms this fact

when he states: "The Institutions of Calvin are so greatly esteemed in England that the book has been most accurately translated into English, and is even fixed in the parish churches for the people to read. Moreover, in each of the two Universities, after the students have finished their circuit in philosophy, as many of them as are designed for the ministry are lectured first of all in that book."

Not only in England, but also in Scotland, was the light kindled from Geneva. John Knox, driven by opposition and intolerance from his native shores, found a refuge in Geneva, and lived there from 1556 to 1559.

Calvin perceived the sterling value of this noble man; and in fact there was very much in common between them. Bold and fearless, yet strong in a majestic wisdom, Knox was the most suitable helper the Genevan Reformer could have had during those three years of his exile.

An intimate friendship was formed between these two men, which continued until the death of Calvin. They were nearly of the same age; and there was a striking similarity between not only their sentiments but also the features of their character. Their esteem was mutual, and the result of it was very fruitful.

On his return to Scotland, Knox was instrumental in establishing the Reformation by the treaty of Leith, in July, 1560; and also of establishing the Presbyterian form of church government, after the Geneva pattern, which has continued to the present day.

The first Confession of Faith was drawn up by Knox; and it is eminently Calvinistic. Eighty-seven years later, in 1647, the Church of Scotland adopted the Westminster Confession of Faith, which was built up by the Independents in 1643.

While living in Geneva, John Knox wrote to his friend Locke: "In my heart I could have wished, yea, and cannot cease to wish, that it might please God to guide and conduct you to this place, where I neither fear nor ashame to say is the most perfect school of Christ that ever was in the earth since the days of the apostles. In other places I confess Christ to be truly preached; but manners and religion to be so sincerely reformed I have not yet seen in any other place beside."

Farel, also, who was well qualified to judge of the state of Geneva, thus writes of its prosperity at this period: "I was lately at Geneva, and so delighted was I that I could scarce tear myself away. I would rather be last in Geneva than first in any other place. Were I not prevented by the Lord, and by my love for my congregation, nothing would hinder me from ending my days there."

The estimate formed by Dr. Thomas M'Crie, not only of the character of John Knox, but also of his relative excellence, is so apt and so valuable that I must make room for it here, as quite within the scope of this chapter: "Knox bore a striking resemblance to Luther in personal intrepidity and in popular eloquence. He approached nearest to Calvin in his religious sentiments, in the severity of his manners, and in a certain impressive air of melancholy which pervaded his character. And he resembled Zwinglius in his ardent attachments to the principles of religious liberty, and in combining his exertions for the reformation of the church with uniform endeavors to improve the political state of the people. Not that I would place our Reformer on a level with this illustrious triumvirate. There is a splendor which surrounds the great German Reformer, partly arising from the intrinsic heroism of his character, and partly reflected from the interesting situation in which his long and doubtful struggle with the court of Rome has placed him in the eyes of Europe, which removes him at a distance from all who started in the same glorious career. The Genevan Reformer surpassed Knox in the extent of his theological learning, and in the unrivalled solidity and clearness of his judgment. And the Reformer of Switzerland, though inferior to him in masculine elocution and in daring courage, excelled him in self-command, in prudence, and in that species of eloquence which steals into the heart, which persuades without irritating, and governs without assuming the tone of authority. But, although 'he attained not to the first three,' I know not, among all the eminent men who appeared at that period, any name which is so well entitled to be placed next to theirs as that of Knox, whether we consider the talents with which he was endowed, or the important services which he performed."

It has thus been shown that the many godly men who were gathered together at Geneva in the providence of God were largely influenced by the teaching of the chief pastor of that city; and that they, like so many streams, conveyed its fertilizing energy to many distant lands. In his Memorials of Archbishop Cranmer, Strype quotes several letters written by that Reformer to Calvin, and the replies of the latter to England, from which, did space permit, many extracts might be made.

Nor must we omit to notice here the immense influence exerted in England by the "Genevan" Bible. After the editions of the Bible known as "Cranmer's," "the Bishops' Bible," and some others, an edition in a smaller (quarto) and more convenient size became extremely popular. This was known, and still is known, as the "Breeches" Bible, from its rendering of the last word in Genesis 3:7; the "Genevan," because translated there; and "Beza's," because of the marginal notes ascribed to him.

This translation became a great favorite here in England, and was only superseded by the "Authorized" Version of 1611. My own copy bears the date 1608. The reader will be pleased to see how Romans 8:28 reads in the "Genevan" Bible: "Also we know that all things worke together for the best unto them that love God, even to them that are called of His purpose."

XVII. The Reformer's Last Days.

After the great victory of the gospel over the Libertines, on September 3rd, 1553, Calvin settled down to much peaceful yet diligent work; but he was never long without molestation from those enemies of all law and propriety. Frequently they interrupted him in preaching; often they insulted him in the streets; and always their influence was in opposition to him. It became necessary for two of them, Bolsec and Castalio, to be banished from Geneva.

The Reformer's warm heart next engaged a band of men to take the gospel to surrounding districts. Of this he writes in a letter to Henry Bullinger, in May, 1561: "It is incredible with what ardor our friends devote themselves to the spread of the gospel. As greedily as men before the pope solicit him for benefices, do they ask for employment in the churches beneath the Cross. They besiege my door to obtain a portion of the field to cultivate. Never had monarch courtiers more eager than mine. They dispute about the stations as if the kingdom of Jesus Christ was peaceably established in France. Sometimes I seek to restrain them. I show to them the atrocious edict which orders the destruction of every house in which Divine service shall have been celebrated. I remind them that in more than twenty towns the faithful have been massacred by the populace."

Those must have been happy days for the preachers, and fruitful days for the gospel. The presence of holy fire within them to stimulate them to service, and the prospect of papal fire to burn them for their service, would put life into their preaching.

It seemed as if Calvin could not prescribe enough work for himself. The responsibilities he undertook, as well as the labors, were immense.

The idea of a college had long been in his mind; and now that there was peace, he proceeded to make the thought a reality. Money was collected, and the new Institution was opened on June 5th, 1559. The inaugural services were held in St. Peter's. After prayer by Calvin, and an address in Latin by Beza, the laws of the college, and the confession to be subscribed by the students, were read. Five masterships or "chairs" were instituted: one of Hebrew, one of Greek, one of philosophy, and two of theology.

The description of this memorial, as given by Bungener, will be full of interest. "After their venerable cathedral, no building is more dear to the Genevese. If you go upstairs to the classrooms, you are in the rooms of the library, full of memorials yet more living and special. There you will be shown the books of Calvin's library, the mute witnesses of his vigils, his sufferings, and his death. There you will turn over the leaves of his manuscripts, deciphering, not without difficulty, a few lines of his feverish writing, rapid as his thoughts. And, if your imagination will but lend itself to the breathing appeals of solitude and silence, there he himself is. You will behold him gliding among those ancient walls, pale, but with a sparkling eye; feeble and sickly, but strong in that inner energy the source of which was in his faith. There also will appear to you, around him, all those of whom he was to be the father: divines, jurists, philosophers, scholars, statesmen, and men of war; all filled with that mighty life which he was to bequeath to the Reformation, after having received it from her. And if you ask the secret of his power, one of the stones of the college will tell it you in a few Hebrew words, which the Reformer had engraved upon it. Come into the court. Enter beneath that old portico which supports the great staircase, and you will read: '*The fear of the Lord is the beginning of wisdom.*' And it is neither on the wall nor on one of the pillars that these words are engraved. Mark well; it is on the keystone. What an emblem! and what a lesson!"

It is not surprising that the studious life of the Reformer, his multiplied labors, and the many fierce storms that had beat upon him, had worn down his strength prematurely. Indeed, the surprise rather is that he had not succumbed years before to toil so arduous as his. He had never been really robust, and in his later years he suffered from quartan ague. At length asthma appeared, attended by spitting of blood, and other disorders. Yet he labored on, and in fact seems to have labored the more as his strength declined. The prudence of this is not our present concern: incessant toil and self-negation were characteristic of the man throughout life.

At this time his charities were great, his hospitality to refugees was extensive, and his personal wants were few. "Satisfied with my humble condition, I have ever delighted in a life of poverty, and am a burden to no one. I remain contented with the office which the Lord has given me." In his last illness he even refused his quarter's salary, saying that he had not earned it.

He preached his last sermon on February 6th, 1564. On that occasion he was seized with so violent a fit of coughing that it brought the blood into his mouth, and stopped his utterance. All his hearers realized too clearly that his last words in public had been spoken.

For four months he suffered extreme prostration, yet continued to labor with his pen. He translated his Harmony on the Pentateuch from Latin into French, revised the translation of Genesis, wrote on the Book of Joshua, and revised his Commentaries on the New Testament. Often during this time a little cold water was his only refreshment.

On March 27th, he was carried to the door of the council-chamber.

Supported by two attendants, he went up the stairs, entered the hall, and proposed a new rector for the school. He thanked the members of the council for all the kindness he had received from them, especially for the friendship they had shown him during this his illness. "I feel that this is the last time that I shall stand here." His farewell moved the council to tears.

On April 2nd, Beza tells us, "it being Easter day, he was carried to church in a chair. He remained during the whole sermon, and received the Sacrament at my hand. He even joined, though with a trembling voice, the congregation in the last hymn: 'Lord, now lettest Thou Thy servant depart in peace.' He was carried out with his face lighted with the joy of Christ."

On April 25th, Calvin made his will. He had only 225 crowns to dispose of; and having done this, and named other small matters, he adds: "I thank God that He has not only had mercy on His poor creature, having delivered me from the abyss of idolatry, but that He has brought me into the clear light of His gospel, and made me a partaker of the doctrine of salvation, of which I was altogether unworthy; yea, that His mercy and goodness have borne so tenderly with my numerous sins and offenses, for which I deserve to be cast from Him and destroyed."

On the 30th April, the Council of Geneva resolved to visit the pastor at his house in the Rue des Chanoines. Raising himself on his bed, he exhorted them ever to maintain inviolate the independence of a city that had been so favored of God. But he reminded them that it was the gospel alone that could fulfill the high destiny of Geneva. "Commending them and Geneva to God," says Beza, "and begging them one and all to pardon him his faults, he held out his hand to them, which they grasped for the last time, and retired as from the death-bed of a father."

On the next day, May 1st, he received the pastors. He exhorted them, in the most affectionate and touching words, to use all holy diligence in their work, to be faithful to their flocks, to be kind one to another, and to maintain the Reformation. For all his failings he asked pardon of God and of them; and finally, adds Beza, "he gave his hand to each, one after the other, which was with such anguish and bitterness of heart in every one, that I cannot even recall it to mind without extreme sadness."

On the next day, May 2nd, he received a letter from

XVII. The Reformer's Last Days.

the aged Farel, now nearly eighty, stating that the writer was just setting out to visit his beloved brother. Calvin penned him this admirable reply: "Farewell, my best and most faithful brother! Since it is the will of God that you should survive me, live in the constant recollection of our union, which, in so far as it was useful to the church of God, will still bear for us abiding fruit in heaven. I wish you not to fatigue yourself on my account. My breath is weak, and I continually expect it to leave me. *It is enough for me that I live and die in Christ, who is gain to His people both in life and death.* Once more, farewell to thee, and to all the brethren thy colleagues."

A few days afterwards Farel, covered with dust, having walked all the way from Neuchatel, entered the chamber of the dying pastor. He had a long interview with him, the particulars of which are not left on record; and on the morrow took his departure.

On the Friday before Whitsunday, May 19th, the pastors were to meet; and Calvin requested that they should do so at his house. When a homely dinner had been prepared, Calvin was carried into the room, and said: "I am come, my brethren, to see you for the last time; for I shall never again sit at table." Then he offered prayer, and tried to eat a little. "But," adds Beza, "before the end of the meal, he requested to be carried back to his chamber, which was close by, saying these words with as cheerful a face as he could command: 'A partition between us will not prevent me, though absent in body, being present with you in spirit.'" During the next few days his flickering life was one continued prayer. On Saturday, May 27th, he seemed to suffer less. At eight o'clock on that evening, death very gently approached him. As he was repeating the words of Paul: *"The sufferings of this present time are not worthy to be compared with the glory to be...,"* those sufferings ceased and glory was revealed. What he could not finish by his failing breath was suddenly realized by his glorified spirit.

The Reformer was buried on the following day, the Lord's day, at two o'clock. The funeral was conducted "in the usual fashion," according to his own wishes;

"not," says Beza, "without many tears." He was buried in a plain coffin, in an ordinary grave, in the Plain-Palais Cemetery outside the town. The historian Ruchat says that "he was buried with all simplicity, in the common cemetery, as he himself had desired; so simply that no one at this day knows where his grave is."

Thus no monument was erected to mark the site; for his monument is nobler and more enduring than any that could have been placed there. The supposed site is now marked by a plain stone, about a foot square, bearing the initials "J. C."

He had lived fifty-four years, ten months, and seventeen days. He died in Beza's arms; and knowing that he deserved his entire confidence, he charged him in his last hours with the duty of editing his correspondence for the use of the church. Beza became Calvin's worthy successor, and was as free from ambition as Calvin himself.

XVIII. Estimate of Calvin's Work.

Any really adequate estimate of the work of a public man must be based upon a knowledge of the circumstances under which he worked and of the times in which he lived. It is hoped that a sufficiently clear view of the surroundings of Calvin's life and of the principles that governed his labors has been set before the reader in the foregoing pages; so that it now only remains to gather up the facts of three-and-a-half centuries ago, and to focus them in the light of the present day.

If by "work" is meant the actual labor accomplished during the lifetime of a man, Calvin's work was immense. It has been said of Samuel Rutherford that, reading his writings, it would appear as if he did nothing but write; hearing him preach, as if he did nothing else but preach. This may with equal point be said of John Calvin. The writing of his *Institutes* would nobly fill an ordinary lifetime; but when his Commentaries are added, covering the whole Bible with the exception of the Book of Revelation, it seems incredible that he could have accomplished both. Then his vast correspondence would seem to demand another lifetime. Above all this, his preaching, expounding, organizing, advising other men and other churches, and his defense of truth, must be taken into account.

But it will be helpful to the reader to have the various branches of the Reformer's life spread out before him in their proper sequence. His work as an Author, as a Preacher, and as a Reformer, will in turn claim our attention.

The *Institutes of the Christian Religion* will stand for

ages as a masterpiece of orderly exposition. Everything is explained with perfect precision. Whether in establishing holy doctrines, in refuting error, or stating truth, this work excels.

One leading excellence of this great "Body of Divinity" is that every doctrine is presented as a part of one undivided whole. A living unity of purpose pervades the entire work. In this the Reformer took up a position that had not been reached by any previous author. Luther and Melancthon had stated and defended truth, and had refuted error, with ability and success; but they had done so piecemeal, so to speak. Calvin's more penetrating and more methodical mind seemed to take in the whole proportion and tendency of truth at one view.

Another leading excellence is the author's universal appeal to the decisions of the Holy Spirit in Scripture. There is no selection of bits of truth out of the Bible to build up a system of his own. He takes the whole written Word as God's one and indivisible declaration of truth, complete and harmonious. Those who think that Calvin invented what is called "Calvinism" are lamentably mistaken; and so long as the *Institutes* are accessible for a few shillings, they are wilfully deceiving themselves and speaking evil of things they do not understand.

A balanced judgment will also realize that, as there are diversities of gifts, so also are there differences in operation; the same Spirit dividing to each severally as He will. We must recognize the wisdom of the words of Luther: "I am born to be a rough controversialist. I clear the ground, pull up weeds, fill up ditches, and smooth the roads. But to build, to plant, to sow, to water, to adorn the country, belongs by the grace of God to Melancthon."

The *Commentaries* on the books of Scripture have been often named in the preceding pages. It may be convenient to state here that a complete set of them consists of forty-eight octavo volumes, with the addition that the Commentary on Romans has been translated by two translators, so making forty-nine. These expositions of the Bible are justly esteemed for their excellency and dignity. There is a profound depth of wisdom, and yet the style is simple. Every word expresses a thought, and has its own place and weight.

The writer's mind bows to the majesty of Scripture, as to the very Word of God; and never refuses to accept what it cannot fathom, on the simple ground that God is the Speaker. Some have thought Calvin inconsistent by reason of this his loyal consistency. While maintaining the absolute sovereignty of God in predestination and election, he at the same time allows Scripture to speak of the freeness of the gospel, of the universal outward call of the gospel, and of the sin of rejecting it: If this is to be inconsistent, then Scripture is inconsistent. His expositions are never cramped by the narrow restrictions of a party; and he never shrinks from giving the real sense of the sacred text. In a word, he called no man Master, but expounded what God has written; and our wisdom will be to imitate him in this.

As an expositor of Scripture, the Word of God was as sacred to him as if he heard it spoken by the lips of its Author. This principle shines in all that he wrote. His expositions stand unrivalled for depth and clearness.

The intense acuteness of his mind enabled him to grasp first principles and essential truths, and he was skillful to place these before his readers.

The letters written by John Calvin form another monument to his memory. There is this remarkable feature about them,—that they are written with the same precision, and with the same ability, as all his other writings. Even when he pleads lack of time in beginning a letter to a friend, he goes on to write with the same care and accuracy as if the whole day were before him. And the number of them is amazing, covering the whole ground from his leaving France to his death in 1564.

It was intended to publish all his available letters in four volumes, in which "at least six hundred" letters would be given. This was undertaken by Dr. Jules Bonnet, transcribing and editing them from the original manuscripts.

But only two of the four volumes were published (1855); and these contain three hundred and thirty-six letters. It is much to be lamented that this undertaking was not completed, as the later letters would have been those of the latest years of the Reformer's life, and therefore the ripest and the best.

As a Preacher, our materials are not sufficient to form a judgment. We have few of his sermons, as such, on record. We can therefore only judge of the character of his preaching by that of his printed works, and by the effects produced by it in Geneva. We rest assured that it was eminently expository, and devoted to the "opening and alleging" (Acts 17:3) of all divine truth. It produced a revolution in Geneva. It is a very significant fact that the building which now stands on the site of the house occupied by Calvin bears over its door the inscription, *Bureau de Salubrite;* that is, Office of Public Health. The teaching of Calvin, even considered apart from its value to the godly, exerted a marvellous moral influence upon Geneva.

As a Reformer, the foregoing pages will have presented a sufficient portrait of Calvin. He stands second to none in the glorious Reformation movement of the sixteenth century. We have traced his influence in England and in other nations. That influence was instrumental in planting more than two thousand Reformed churches in France. But it was in Geneva especially that he unfolded the energies of his ardent spirit. He was there the light of the church, the strength of the laws, the restorer of morals, and the fountain of literature. To this day Switzerland is reaping what he sowed; so that Montesquieu remarks: "The Genevese ought to bless the moment of the birth of Calvin, and that of his arrival within their walls."

XIX. Estimate of Calvin's Character.

This chapter has not been prepared without a perusal of those estimates of Calvin that have been written by his avowed enemies and opponents. It is of immense importance to any public man to know what his enemies say of him. It is highly desirable to know both sides of any case of controversy; for the simple reason that the man who knows nothing of the other side knows very little of his own.

Dr. J. M. Mason writes: "Had anything been wanting in his own writings to evince the greatness of this extraordinary man, it would have been supplied by the rancorous malignity which assailed him during his life, and which has been hardly, if at all, abated by his death."

When, therefore, biographers make use of such terms as they are not ashamed of coming in order to blacken the name of Calvin, we need not hesitate to appraise them at their true value. There were several defects in the character of Calvin; and these were just the excesses of his virtues. To illustrate this, we may quote that Bucer wrote to blame the Reformer for his extreme vehemence. To this complaint Calvin replied: "My struggles are not greater against my vices, which are very great and numerous, than against my impatience; and my efforts are not wholly useless. I have not, however, been able yet to conquer that ferocious animal."

No one can read the letters written by Calvin without feeling that he was a most *tender-hearted* man. I place this feature of his character first because the contrary has been assumed by ill-informed persons. Take the following extract from a letter written to Knox on the occasion of the death of his wife: "Your loss is a deep and bitter affliction to me. You had a wife to whom few could be compared; but you know well where to find consolation, and I doubt not that you will bear this great sorrow with patience. Greet the faithful brethren in my name."

Here is an extract from a letter to Goodman on the same: "I grieve not a little that our brother Knox has been deprived of his most sweet *(suavissima)* wife. But I rejoice that, afflicted as he has been, he has continued to labor strenuously for Christ and the church."

In the light of such letters, those who speak of the "ferocity" of Calvin simply proclaim their utter ignorance of the man. A hundred extracts could be given.

The Reformer's character was also marked by *a straightforward honest decision*. It is well-known that he loved Philip Melancthon, and that on more than one occasion he conceded to Philip as much as his conscience permitted. But he well knew where to draw the line, as the following will show. I extract it from a letter from Calvin to Melancthon, dated June 18th, 1550: "Several things which you think indifferent are obviously repugnant to the Word of God. Truly, if I have any understanding in divine things, you ought not to have made such large concessions to the papists; partly because you have loosed what the Lord has bound in His Word, and partly because you have afforded *occasion for bringing insult upon the gospel*. Lest you may perhaps have forgotten what I once said to you, I now remind you of it: namely, that we consider *our ink* too precious if we hesitate to bear our testimony in writing to those things which so many of the flock are daily sealing with *their blood*. Although I am fully persuaded that the fear of death never compelled you in the very least to swerve from the right path, yet I am apprehensive that it is just possible that another species of fear may have proved too much for your courage; for I know how greatly you are horrified at the charge of rude severity."

This letter is so admirably worded that we must marvel at its almost severe faithfulness and its tender love. To give any real "occasion for bringing insult upon the gospel" was abhorrent to Calvin, even in so dear a friend as Melancthon; and therefore it called for this sharp reproof. And the sentence in which "our ink" is placed in apposition to "their blood" is worthy of the noblest pen that ever wrote.

Perhaps the most prominent feature in Calvin's character was his *love of work*. He could not bear to be idle for a moment.

Of this Dr. Hoyle writes: "What shall I say of his indefatigable industry, almost beyond the power of nature; which, set against our loitering will, I fear, exceed all credit? It may be the truest object of admiration, how one lean, worn, spent, and wearied body could hold out. He gave, every week of the year through, three divinity lectures. Every other week, over and above, he preached every day; so that I know not whether more to admire his constancy or theirs that heard him. Some have reckoned that his yearly lectures were one hundred and eighty-six, and his yearly sermons two hundred and eighty-six. Every Thursday he sat in the presbytery. Every Friday, when the ministers met to consult upon difficult texts, he made as good as a lecture. Besides all this, there was scarce a day that exercised him not in answering the doubts and questions of different churches and pastors. Scarcely a year passed wherein some volume came not forth."

Let us hear what Beza says of his untiring diligence: "In the year 1562 it might already be seen that Calvin was hastening with rapid strides to a better world. He ceased not, however, to comfort the afflicted, to exhort, even to preach, and to give lectures. The following year his sufferings so increased that it was difficult to conceive how so weak a body, and exhausted as it had been by labor and sickness, could retain so strong and mighty a spirit. But even now he could not be induced to spare himself; for when he was obliged, against his will, to leave the public duties of his office unfulfilled, he was employed at home, giving advice to those who sought him, or wearing out his amanuenses by dictating to them his works and letters. When we besought him to refrain at least during his sickness from dictating and writing, he answered, 'Would you that the Lord should find me idle when He comes?' The year 1564 was the first of his eternal rest, and the beginning for us of a long and justifiable grief."

Calvin was also not without *meekness* and *humility*. I have only space for two instances. A good deal of trouble had been given in Geneva by Troillet, who was unworthy of the position to which he aspired. But when death laid his finger on this man, he sent for the pastor he had so abused and wronged. Calvin hastened to the dying man, forgave him, and comforted him.

He has been charged with fierceness and bigotry. The charge comes with ill grace from the lips that speak it. When disputes ran high between Luther and some other Reformers concerning the manner of Christ's presence in the bread and wine, Luther, whose temper was naturally warm, heaped many hard names upon those who differed from him. Calvin came in for his share of this. In a letter to Henry Bullinger he says: — "I hear that Luther has at length published an atrocious invective, not so much against you as against us all. In these circumstances I can scarcely venture to ask for your silence; since it is unjust that the innocent should be thus attacked without having an opportunity to clear themselves; although it is at the same time difficult to decide whether that would be expedient. But I hope you will remember in the first place how great a man Luther is, and in how many excellent endowments he excels; with what fortitude and constancy, with what dexterity and efficacious learning, he has hitherto applied himself, both to overthrow the kingdom of Antichrist, and to spread the doctrine of salvation. It is a frequent saying with me that, if Luther should even call me a devil, my veneration for him is notwithstanding so great that I shall ever acknowledge him to be an illustrious servant of God, who, though he abounds in extraordinary virtues, yet labors under great imperfections. I wish he would endeavor to restrain the violence with which he boils over on all occasions; and that he would always direct the vehemence which is nat-

XIX. Estimate of Calvin's Character.

ural to him against the enemies of truth, and not brandish it also against the servants of the Lord. I should be glad if he took more pains in searching out his own defects. Flatterers have done him much harm, especially as he is by nature too much inclined to self-indulgence; but it is our duty, whilst we reprehend what is bad in him, to make due allowance for his excellent qualities. I beg therefore of you and your colleagues, in the first place to consider that you have to deal with a distinguished servant of Christ, to whom we are all much indebted; and in the next, that all you will obtain by a conflict will be to afford sport to the ungodly, and a triumph over ourselves as well as over the gospel; for if we indulge in mutual abuse, they will be but too ready to believe both sides."

This admirable letter reveals much good sense. How true his remarks are with regard to controversy, experience and observation agree to prove. In most controversies, even in the case of those who contend for truth, self-opinion takes the place of self-judgment, and natural heat and vindictiveness occupy the throne instead of the Word of God.

Let not mortal praise be given to any man above his desert, or even beyond what he would accept. God alone can create; a man is only great when God sees fit to accomplish anything great by his instrumentality.

Never did any man understand this better than Calvin. It seemed natural to him, and was certainly no effort to him, to refer all back to God. There is absolutely nothing in all his two thousand and seventy letters to indicate that he was ever tempted to appropriate the smallest portion of human praise to himself. Luther, in more than one place, complacently dwells on the thought that he, a little monk, has made the papal throne to tremble and so well stirred the whole papal system. But Calvin never says anything like this; he never even seems to have the thought of it occur to him. Everywhere we find underlying all he wrote the thought that God alone is all and does all, "It was more God's work than mine," he says of the birth of his *Institutes*.

Ernest Renan, educated for the Romish priesthood, but later a sceptic, pays this striking tribute to Calvin's character: — "Calvin was one of those absolute men, cast complete in one mold, who is taken in wholly at a single glance: one letter, one action, suffices for a judgment of him. There were no folds in that inflexible soul, which never knew doubt or hesitation. Careless of wealth, of titles, of honors, indifferent to pomp, modest in his life, transparently humble, sacrificing everything to the desire of making others like himself, I hardly know of a man, save Ignatius Loyola, who could match him.... Lacking that vivid, deep, sympathetic ardor which was one of the secrets of Luther's success, lacking the charm, the languishing tenderness of Francis of Sales, Calvin succeeded, in an age and in a country which called for a reaction towards Christianity, simply because he was the most Christian man of his generation."

Guizot, the French historian, thus concludes his biography: "Calvin is great by reason of his marvelous powers, his enduring labors, and the moral height and purity of his character. Earnest in faith, pure in motive, austere in his life, and mighty in his works, Calvin is one of those who deserve their great fame. Three centuries separate us from him, but it is impossible to examine his character and history without feeling, if not affection and sympathy, at least profound respect and admiration for one of the great Reformers of Europe and one of the great Christians of France."

It will now be desirable to give the rapid sketch of Calvin's character written by his intimate friend and successor, Theodore Beza. It is hardly possible to curtail it. "Calvin was not of large stature: his complexion was pale, and rather brown: even to his last moments his eyes were peculiarly bright, and indicative of his penetrating genius. He knew nothing of luxury in his outward life, but was fond of the greatest neatness, as became his thorough simplicity. His manner of living was so arranged that he showed himself equally averse to extravagance and meanness. He took so little nourishment, such being the weakness of his stomach, that for many years he contented himself with one meal a day. Of sleep he had almost none. His memory was incredible; he immediately recognized, after many years, those whom he had once seen; and when he had been interrupted for several hours, in some work about which he was employed, he could immediately resume and continue it, without reading again what he had written. Of the numerous details connected with the business of his office, he never forgot even the most trifling, and this notwithstanding the multitude of his affairs. His judgment was so acute and correct in regard to the most opposite concerns about which his advice was asked, that he often seemed to possess the gift of looking into the future. I never remember to have heard that anyone who followed his counsel went wrong. He despised fine speaking, and was rather abrupt in his language; but he wrote admirably, and no theologian of his time expressed himself so clearly, so impressively and acutely as he; and yet he labored as much as any one of his contemporaries, or of the fathers. For this fluency he was indebted to the several studies of his youth, and to the natural acuteness of his genius, which had been still further increased by the practice of dictation, so that proper and dignified expressions never failed him, whether he was writing or speaking. He never, in any wise, altered the doctrine which he first adopted, but remained true to it to the last.

"Although nature had endowed Calvin with a dignified seriousness, both in manner and character, no one was more agreeable than he in ordinary conversation. He could bear, in a wonderful manner, with the failings of others, when they sprang from mere weakness. Thus he never shamed anyone by ill-timed reproofs, or discouraged a weak brother; while, on the other hand, he never spared or overlooked willful sin. An enemy to all flattery, he hated dissimulation, especially every dishonest sentiment in reference to religion. He was therefore as powerful and strong an enemy to vices of this kind as he was a devoted friend to truth, simplicity and uprightness. His temperament was naturally choleric, and his active public life had tended greatly to increase this failing; but the Spirit of God had so taught him to moderate his anger, that no word ever escaped him unworthy of a righteous man. Still less did he ever commit aught unjust towards others. It was then only, indeed, when the question concerned religion, and when he had to contend against hardened sinners, that he allowed himself to be moved and excited beyond the bounds of moderation.

"Let us take but a single glance at the history of those men who, in any part of the world, have been distinguished for their virtues, and no one will be surprised at finding that the great and noble qualities which Calvin exhibited, both in his private and public life, excited against him a host of enemies. We ought not indeed to feel any wonder that so powerful a champion of pure doctrine, and so stern a teacher of sound morals, as well at home as in the world, should be so fiercely assailed. Rather ought we to let our admiration dwell on the fact that, standing alone as he did, he was sufficiently mighty to avail himself of that strongest of weapons, the Word of God. Thus, however numerous the adversaries which Satan excited against him (for he never had any but such as had declared war against piety and virtue), the Lord gave His servant sufficient strength to gain the victory over all.

"Having been for sixteen years a witness of his labors, I have pursued the history of his life and death with all fidelity; and I now unhesitatingly testify that every true Christian may find in this man the noble pattern of a truly Christian life and Christian death; a pattern, however, which it is as easy to calumniate as it would be difficult to follow."

It may be asked whether we should consider the aims of a man who wielded power so great and exerted an influence so powerful were dictated by personal ambition, or inspired by zeal for the honor and glory of God.

There can be but one answer to such a question. Though the charge of ambition was brought against him, and is still believed by some, it cannot bear the light of historic facts. His "ambition" was that of the apostle who labored so that he might be approved of his Master, and accepted of Him.

To these testimonials only one more must be selected,—from the pen of Professor Dorner, of Berlin: "Calvin was equally great in intellect and character, lovely in social life, full of tender sympathy and faithfulness to friends, yielding and forgiving towards personal offenses, but inexorably severe when he saw the honor of God obstinately and malignantly attacked. He combined French fire and practical good sense with German depth and soberness."

XX. WHAT THE REFORMATION REALLY MEANS.

What the Reformation really means is simply Re-formation: that is, the decay and removal of a previous system of unreal and false religion to make room for that which is real and true. The word itself is used once in Scripture (Hebrews 9:10), where it is stated that the rites and ceremonies of the old covenant were "imposed on them until the time of *re*-formation." The new covenant, therefore, has superseded the old. All believers are priests unto God, and are privileged to draw near in full assurance of faith, without the interposition of any human "priest" or mediator.

In order to make this very clear and plain, I am going to make a quotation from an authoritative Roman Catholic source. There is now being published a [Roman] "Catholic Encyclopaedia," to be completed in fifteen volumes. The third volume bears date 1908. Each article in this work has the signature of some writer of eminence in the Roman Church. The three volumes thus far issued bear the *imprimatur* of Archbishop John M. Finlay, of New York. The three quotations I shall make are taken from two articles, on Calvin and on Calvinism, each signed by Canon "William Barry," of Leamington.

Writing first on John Calvin, Canon Barry says (page 195): "This man, undoubtedly the greatest of Protestant divines, and perhaps, after St. Augustine, the most perseveringly followed by his disciples of any Western writer on theology, was born at Noyon....Luther's eloquence made him popular by its force, humor, rudeness, and vulgar style. Calvin spoke to the learned at all times, even when preaching before multitudes. His manner is classical; he reasons on system; he has little humor; instead of striking with a cudgel he uses the weapons of a deadly logic and persuades by a teacher's authority, not by a demagogue's calling of names. He gives articulate expression to the principles which Luther had stormily thrown out upon the world in his vehement pamphleteering; and the *Institutes,* as they were left by their author, have remained ever since the standard of orthodox Protestant belief in all the churches known as Reformed."

I now quote from the same writer on Calvinism: "To the modern world, however, Calvin stands peculiarly for the Reformation; his doctrine is supposed to contain the essence of the gospel; and multitudes who reject Christianity mean merely the creed of Geneva. Why does this happen? Because, we answer, Calvin gave himself out as following closely in the steps of St. Paul and St. Augustine. The Catholic teaching at Trent he judged to be semi-Pelagian, a stigma which his disciples fix especially on Jesuit schools, above all, on Molina. Hence the curious situation arises, that, while the Catholic consent of the East and West finds little or no acknowledgment as an historical fact among assailants of religion the views which a single Reformer enunciated are taken as though representing the New Testament. In other words, a highly refined individual system, not traceable as a whole to any previous age, supplants the public teaching of centuries. Calvin, who hated scholasticism, comes before us, as Luther had already done, in the shape of a scholastic. His 'pure doctrine' is gained by appealing, not to tradition, the 'deposit' of faith, but to argument in abstract terms exercised upon Scripture. He is neither a critic nor a historian. He takes the Bible as something given; and he manipulates the Apostles' Creed in accordance with his own ideas. The *Institutes* are not a history of dogma, but a treatise, only not to be called an essay because of its peremptory tone.

"Calvin annihilates the entire space, with all its developments, which lies between the death of St. John and the sixteenth century. He does indeed quote St. Augustine, but he leaves out all that Catholic foundation on which the Doctor of Grace built.

"One sweeping consequence of the Reformation is yet to be noticed. As it denied the merit of good works even in the regenerate, all those Catholic beliefs and ordinances which implied a Communion of Saints actively helping each other by prayer and self-sacrifice were flung aside. Thus Purgatory, Masses for the dead, invocation of the blessed in heaven, and their intercession for us, are scouted by Calvin as 'Satan's devices.' A single argument gets rid of them all: do they not make void the Cross of Christ our only Redeemer?"

We have here, from a Roman Catholic pen, a very plain and lucid view of the vital difference between the two religions,—man's and God's. "He takes the Bible as something given." Blessed be its heavenly Author and Explainer, we *do* take the infallible Word as given by God to every humble learner. And we say of all teaching that is not consonant with its pages of light and grace, let it be "swept away," let it be "flung aside," let it be "scouted" as unworthy of our regard.

As to the "merit of good works, even in the regenerate," those who really are regenerate are the most able to form an opinion. Taught by the Spirit who inspired the Word, we say of our best works, and of our worst works, let them be "swept away," let them be "flung aside," let them be "scouted" altogether. The only merits we desire to know are those of our Redeemer, the Friend of sinners.

With regard to purgatory, we do indeed bridge over the entire interval between the death of John and the twentieth century, and we go back to the Word of God. In that Book we seek in vain for the remotest semblance of anything like the purgatory taught by the Church of Rome. We therefore consider the error worthy to be "swept away," to be "flung aside," and to be "scouted," with heart, and soul, and strength. Jesus has "by Himself purged our sins" (Hebrews 1:3) by washing us "in His own blood" (Revelation 1:4), "having obtained eternal redemption for us" (Hebrews 9:12). This is a sweet purgatory to a sinner taught of God: he needs and knows no other.

Masses for the dead; invocation of so-called saints; and their intercession for sinners on earth: what are these but denials of the finished work of Jesus? We can but pity the poor deluded and mistaken souls that hide under these "refuges of lies," and build upon such fatal quicksands.

We heartily and earnestly invite such to read the Word for themselves, in the hope that, taught by the Spirit of God, they also will be enabled to "sweep away," to "fling aside," and to "scout" these delusions. *"A single argument gets rid of them all: do they not make void the Cross of Christ, our only Redeemer?"* I cannot but marvel that a Roman Catholic pen should write a sentence so eminently Scriptural. Indeed a single argument is all that is needed: *the Cross of Christ.* There, and in His empty tomb, is the death of all human merit, all condemnation, all curse; the payment of all penalty; the justification of the ungodly; the pardon of the vilest sinner who by a Divinely-wrought faith believes in Jesus. *And this is what is meant by the Reformation.* Taught by Luther, by Calvin, by Wycliffe, by Zwingli, by Knox, by Farel; by our Reformers and martyrs; and by an army of God-anointed teachers "from the death of John to this twentieth century,"— this is the grand single argument that *"sweeps away"* all that makes void the Word of God. And if "a single argument gets rid of them all," then let us acknowledge that we need no other. Let us take our stand with—not merely John Calvin, nor merely Augustine, but with one who bore in his body the branding marks of the Lord Jesus (Galatians 6:14-17), and say with him: "But God forbid that I should glory, save in the cross of our Lord Jesus Christ."

In bringing to a close this all too short life of the Reformer, there remains one fact to be recorded which might well have found a place on an earlier page. It is the fact that there was another Jean Cauvin, also at Noyon; and that the evil life of this man has by some writers been brought against the Reformer. Thus Dr. D'Aubigne says: "We know what the popish writers are accustomed to do. They take advantage of the misdeeds of Jean Cauvin at Noyon, and ascribe them to the Reformer. They tell their readers gravely that he was driven from his native town for misconduct, after having been condemned to be scourged and even branded."

Thus we read in Scripture of two disciples bearing the name Judas. One of them was "not Iscariot" (John 14:22): the other betrayed the Lord, and died by his own hand after confession to the priests.

The facts of the case are very simple, and may be briefly stated. Some years after Calvin had left Noyon, another man of the same name arrived in that town from another part of France. He was at first made a member of the choir, and afterwards had a chapel set apart for his use. But it was not long before his disorderly life excited alarm among his friends. He was reprimanded, punished, and even deprived of his stipend; but to this he paid no attention. At length he was expelled from his position and from the town.

The dean of Noyon is careful to add that *this* Jean Cauvin died a good Catholic. "Thanks be to God that he never turned his coat nor changed his religion."

This remarkable confession proves that all that has been written against *the* John Calvin is false. It also shamelessly states that a wicked man who never changes his religion is a better Catholic than a godly man who leads a blameless life.

But I am able to quote the latest *authoritative* testimony on this matter, from the same volume named at the beginning of this chapter, and also from the pen of Canon Barry (Catholic Encyclopaedia, vol. 3, p. 196): "Calvin had never been an ardent Catholic; but the stories told at one time of his ill-regulated conduct have no foundation."

XXI. Our Present Position, Privilege, and Duty.

The present trend of events in the world of religion can only be understood by consulting the infallible chart of Scripture. Thereon, with a divine accuracy, depicted all that will take place to the end of time, with all the changes that are merely the ripples on the ocean surface.

The germ of every error may be clearly seen in the question asked in the garden: "Yea, hath God said?" in the third of Genesis. And the germ of all truth is in the Lord's own declaration in the third of John: "Ye must be born again." All the conflicts between hell and heaven are waged around these two standards; and the war is fierce and incessant. Our own individual position on this battleground is a matter of supreme and vital importance.

By whatever distinctive temporary names the combatants are known, and however varied the colors and shapes of the small flags seen in the war, there are only two armies. However varying the apparent successes and defeats of either side, the final victory is determined and certain. It is in fact already won. The wilderness of temptation, Gethsemane, Calvary, the open tomb, have foreviewed the assured issue; and the gates of heaven have received the crowned Conqueror. The all-important thing now, therefore, is to be under the banner that already has victory inscribed upon it.

The present time is one of disintegration, unrest, and rapid change. Each event of today occurs with a rapidity unknown in former days. Systems of religion, forms of belief, human organizations, crumble into dust to give place to others newly-born. With an increased circulation of Holy Scripture, and in one sense an increasing knowledge of it, has grown a tacit denial of its Divine Authorship. The owl dares to deny the supremacy of the mid-day sun; the penknife (Jeremiah 36:23) lifts itself up against the two-edged sword (Hebrews 4:12). This word, which is a "critic" of the thoughts and intents of the heart, is criticized by the darkened understanding of man. This "criticism" may be "higher" or lower; but it is of necessity atheism in its inception and in its fruit. It may be disguised as "freedom of thought and enquiry"; but it is most miserable bondage and slavery. The principle at its root is discernible in each of its assumed features.

It may be that the discontinuance of Catechisms and Confessions of Faith have helped this downward movement; it may be an effect rather than a cause. What is certain is that an intelligent grasp of essential Divine truths is less common than formerly; and this is much to be regretted. There may be a danger in being thus indoctrinated from childhood into a "system" of truth, inasmuch as no system can possibly embrace the whole of truth; but there is another danger to be avoided on the other side. The only complete and perfect creed is the entire Word of God. Dr. Horatius Bonar was not the only humble disciple who longed for this "perfect creed" and yearned for this "scholarship of heaven." Every loyal servant of his Master, every faithful warrior under His standard, familiar daily with temptation, toil, defeat, and victory desires to know all truth in its influence on life and fruit.

If therefore a "system of truth," whether called a Catechism, a Confession, or a Creed, may sometimes involve a partial view of what God has revealed, yet, rightly held, loved, and practiced, it certainly builds up character. It was here that John Calvin excelled. His *Institutes* form a grand repository of truths, logically deduced from Scripture, and forming one harmonious whole—a Confession, a Creed, a fundamental Basis of belief.

His *Commentaries* open those truths, and take the reader by the hand through all the treasure-houses. Dry bones may make a skeleton; but the living body cannot fight without bones. Creed makes character; and character wins the victory.

It is our priceless privilege to enjoy the heritage committed to us by the Reformers, the Martyrs, the Teachers of former days; and not merely to enjoy it, but to hold it as a sacred trust. They shed their blood to secure our inheritance to us; and it were a shameful betrayal of our trust to hold it loosely. To them, under God, we are indebted for our liberty of conscience, our national greatness, our open Bibles. If "righteousness exalteth a nation" (Proverbs 14:34), then verily a fatal Nemesis awaits the nation that builds its throne upon a lie. Let Italy, and Spain, and other Roman Catholic ruins tell us to tell our children the meaning of bondage, darkness, decay, and death. The only supremacy worthy the name is that of truth and light. The only liberty is that of the Word of God, the truth that makes the freeman.

Perhaps the most ominous feature of today is the decay of a sturdy Protestant feeling in the face of a stealthy and underground advance of the designs of Romanist; the apathy and indifference that says it matters not.

It is surely not for the stability of our throne to alter the Coronation Oath.

It cannot be any bulwark to our shores to allow the agents of Rome, with unlimited wealth at command, to secure the best estates of old England for the purposes of the papacy. It cannot contribute to our national honor to allow the imprisonment of women in the darkness of nunneries, and to forbid the light of heaven to shine into those houses of bondage. Why the apathy of the average Briton as he sees these things? Is it that God has judicially poured upon us a spirit of slumber? Is it that He intends to take us at our word, and allow us to squander our priceless inheritance? If so, let us instruct our dear children to be ready for darker days than England has yet seen, and for a struggle far more strenuous than girded our forefathers to the war.

The last sentence has recalled to mind another grave danger that is ever present. I refer here to the tampering with history in our educational books. It is the fact that in many of these the Reformation is called a blunder or a crime; and that contempt is suggested towards our glorious martyrs. I will quote one instance out of many,—from the "Cambridge Modern History," Volume 2, pages 537 and 538, occurring in a chapter by J. B. Mullinger, M.A.: "The social eminence, high character, and personal popularity of not a few of the English martyrs, unalloyed, as in many cases these qualities were, with political disaffection, served to invest their fate with a peculiar interest in the eyes of their fellow-countrymen,—an interest which Foxe's *Book of Martyrs,* chained to the 'eagle-brass' of many a parish church, did much to perpetuate. The prominence thus secured for that partial record was the means of winning for its contents an amount of attention from later historical writers greatly in excess of its actual merits."

Let every parent read the last sentence through twice, very slowly; and then resolve to examine every educational book placed in the hands of the children he loves. "Privilege" and "responsibility" are the two ways of spelling the same fact. Our duty is to "hold" and "hold fast" and "hold forth" the living truth of God to the uttermost of our love and of our energy. For, although the victory is assured, it is only assured to those who fight. Controversy about forms and words is waste of strength in this warfare: controversy such as God asks us for is nine-tenths prayer, and is certain of success.

Profession of truth, whether more or less "Calvinistic," if alone, will fade either at death or at an earlier date; confession of truth, in heart and life, in word and deed, in storm and stress and conflict to the death,—*this is victory.*

May it be the happy lot of reader and writer to have it said of him at the last, as Theodore Beza said of John Calvin: *"He endured, as seeing Him who is invisible."*

CPSIA information can be obtained
at www.ICGtesting.com
Printed in the USA
LVHW091317061020
668094LV00002B/480